THE AIRPORT SITE: A MULTICOMPONENT SITE IN THE SANGAMON RIVER DRAINAGE

by

Donna C. Roper

Illinois State Museum
Research Series, Papers in Anthropology, No. 4

Illinois State Museum
Springfield, Illinois
1978

Printed by Authority of the State of Illinois
(P.O. 7225—1M—8-78)
ISSN 0095-2915
ISBN 0-89792-074-0

TABLE OF CONTENTS

FIGURES

TABLES

PLATES

ACKNOWLEDGMENTS

I wish to thank Mr. Russell R. Pankey, Airport Manager and Director of Operations, and the Springfield Airport Authority Board of Commissioners for permitting and funding the Airport Site excavations. I thank also the Illinois State Museum Society for supporting me during both the fieldwork and the analysis. I am grateful to Michelle Millot and Jean Sparks for typing several drafts of the manuscript.

Walter E. Klippel secured the contract and was overall director of the Airport Site Project. I would like to thank him as well as R. Bruce McMillan and Stanley A. Ahler for advice and commentary during the fieldwork. Linda Klepinger visited the excavations and offered advice on excavating and recording burials; James E. King generously provided a sufficient supply of preservative to treat the poorly preserved bone; and Judi Johnson kept the accounts straight and the crew paid.

The summer of 1974 provided either cold, drizzly forty-degree or hot, humid one-hundred-degree weather—nothing else. Somehow the crew took it all in stride. My greatest thanks are extended to Vida Leong, Kathie Cullen, Dean Turner, Dave Johnson, Debbie Pelham, Ken Shun Bill Weedman, and Tom Gephart—all of whom were employed for at least part of the duration; and also to Bob Samis, Louis Browning, Fran King, Dave Miller, Rose Shun, Andy Christenson, and several members of Walter Klippel's "Anthropology and Archaeology of Central Illinois" class at Lincoln Land Community College—all of whom volunteered their time.

DCR

Plate 1. The Airport Site. *Above:* Looking northwest along the ridge on which the site is located. *Below:* Till plain topography to the southwest of the site.

THE AIRPORT SITE: A MULTICOMPONENT SITE
IN THE SANGAMON RIVER DRAINAGE

INTRODUCTION

The Titterington Focus was originally designated in 1950 for a group of mortuary sites in the St. Louis area in Illinois and Missouri. Since its first mention (Titterington 1950), several related habitation sites have been excavated and reported (Klippel 1969; n.d.; Houart 1971:31–34; Cook n.d.), and information on this and similar material in Missouri has been summarized (C. Chapman 1975); but only one other report on a mortuary site has appeared (Bacon and Miller 1957).

In the spring of 1974, it was learned that proposed expansion of taxiway facilities at Capital Airport, Springfield, Illinois, would necessitate the relocation of a county road and that the relocated road would pass directly over an archaeological site recorded two years prior. Upon initial survey in 1972, the site had yielded a large biface, diagnostic of the Titterington Focus. Additionally, fragments of bone and human teeth and portions of several other bifaces were found during preliminary surface examination of the site, all suggesting that the Airport Site was a mortuary component of the Titterington Focus.

As of spring 1974, the Airport Site was the only site known in the Sangamon Valley with Titterington material. Since the Titterington Focus is poorly known, the site was considered important for understanding not only Sangamon Valley prehistory but also for understanding more about the Late Archaic period in central Illinois.

Further, initial surface collections suggested that the site was probably multicomponent and multifunctional. The study of subsistence/settlement patterns is a major focus of archaeological activity, both in Illinois in general (e.g., Struever 1968; Winters 1969) and in the Sangamon River valley in particular (e.g., Klippel 1972a; Roper 1975). Such studies frequently concentrate on major habitation sites with a high debris density and a wide variety of artifact classes. Little attention is given to the related "limited activity" sites. Yet these small, shallow, light debris density sites are integral parts of the settlement systems of prehistoric groups (e.g., Plog 1974, Anderson 1975) as well as of ethnographically documented societies (e.g., Campbell 1968). Although such sites are rarely deep, inferences concerning their role in the settlement system of prehistoric societies are possible. If a general functional approach is used, the examination of such sites and a comparison with their deeper, more productive counterparts can provide a far more complete synthesis of a group's settlement system.

Accordingly, permission to excavate the Airport Site and funds for a Phase 2 excavation were sought from and granted by the Springfield Airport Authority Board of Commissioners. Fieldwork was carried out in the summer of 1974 under the general direction of Walter E. Klippel and under the direct supervision of the writer.

THE SITE

The Airport Site, 11Sg^{v}280, is in the north quadrant of Capital Airport, Springfield, Illinois. Its legal location is the NW¼ SE¼ NE¼ Section 8 T16N R5W in Sangamon County.

The landscape of the Springfield area was shaped by events of the Pleistocene. Four times the glaciers advanced and retreated; twice they covered the area; a third time they stopped short of it but nevertheless exerted a tremendous impact on the character of the river valley. During the Illinoian Stage (the third major glacial advance of the Pleistocene and the second to cover the Springfield area), grinding action of the glaciers created a very flat till plain (Willman and Frye 1970:27). During the latter part of this stage, the Sangamon River drainage system itself was formed (Miller 1973:1). During the succeeding Wisconsinan Stage (the last of the four major Pleistocene glacial advances), the glaciers stopped short of the Springfield area, but winds deposited a thick blanket of loess in front of the ice. Glacial melting further caused increased discharge through the Sangamon River channel, and aeolian sand deposits were formed on the bluffs. It is on one such sandy area that the Airport Site is located.

The site is on the top of a sandy ridge (Pl. 1), oriented northwest-southeast (Fig. 1). To the south of the site, the landscape gives way to the flat Illinoian age till plain (Pl. 1). To the north, the bluff drops gently down into the Sangamon River bottoms. The soil of the ridge is classed as Alvin-Lamont Sandy Loam, a moderately permeable, acidic soil found on long, narrow ridges over aeolian sand deposits (unpublished maps, U.S.D.A. Soil Conservation Service). The loose sandy soil would have been easily dug by prehistoric peoples. However, its acidity does not

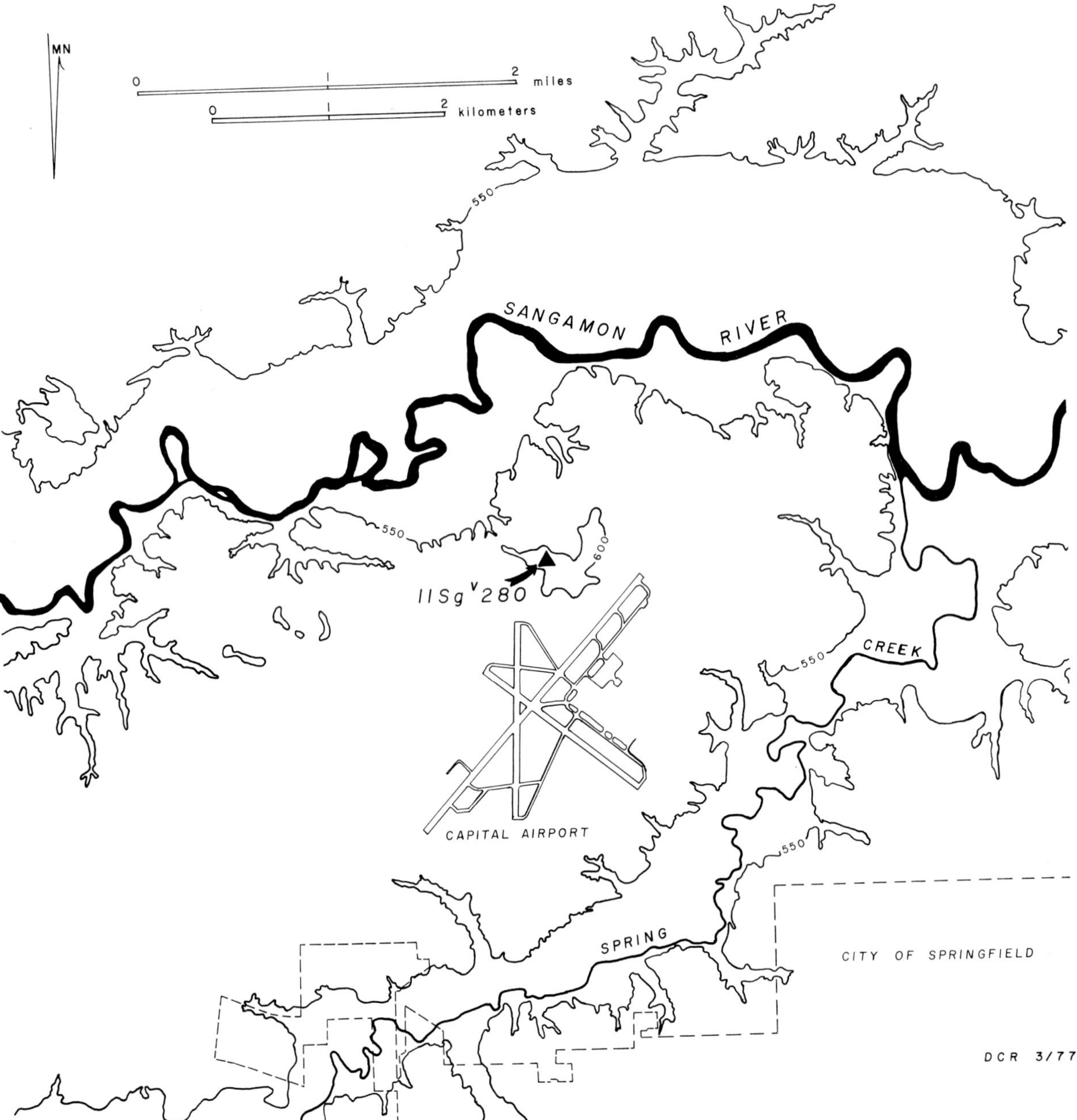

Fig 1. Location of the Airport Site.

facilitate good bone preservation. A map of the early 19th century vegetation shows a cover of deciduous forest whose numerically dominant elements were Black Oak, White Oak, Hickory, and Elm (Johnson 1972). If the 19th century vegetation records can be applied to the Late Archaic period, the Airport Site would be within this forest near the edge. The central Illinois plains were largely prairie-covered. Indications from both soil and vegetation maps are that the site was within about 200 meters of the prairie/forest ecotone.

Except for the right-of-way for the county road that now crosses the site location, the ridge is under cultivation. Repeated plowing and disking over the years, exposing bone, chipped-stone debris, and rock on the ground surface, led to the discovery of the site, but it also disturbed the skeletal material and associated artifacts.

INVESTIGATIONS

Prior to the intensive fieldwork which forms the basis of this report, the Airport Site was visited twice. Casual surface collections were made on both occasions. The site was visited again after fieldwork and after construction of the county road relocation. Casual surface collections were also made at that time. Surface material collected on these occasions is included in the present analysis.

The major fieldwork was carried out from 25 May to 29 July 1974, although heavy rains during the first month severely hampered field operations by either directly raining out the day or rendering the surface unworkable.

A site datum was established off the edge of the right-of-way, 32°47′ southeast of and 37.8 m (124 ft) away from Road Station 45+0. This datum was designated 666N 666W of the actual but arbitrary datum. A base line was extended west from this point using a farmer's level, and a grid of three-meter squares was imposed on the site by taping and triangulation. All squares were designated by the coordinates of their southeast corner.

An intensive surface collection (cf. Redman and Watson 1970) was carried out in June. Ideally, such collections should be carried out prior to excavations, but at the time excavations were started, the field had been recently disked and needed several good rains before surface collection was feasible. Therefore, collection was delayed until after rains improved visibility of surface debris. By this time, several squares had been opened and others were under back-dirt piles. The area within the right-of-way of the

road was gridded off in three-meter squares. All debris on the surface of each unit was collected and bagged, each bag labeled with the square's grid coordinates. A total of 244 units, or 2,196 square meters, was collected in this manner in approximately six hours with a crew of six. An additional 126 units, or 1,134 square meters, were laid out and collected along the ridge to the northwest of the right-of-way. In all, 370 units, or 3330 square meters, were collected (Fig. 2).

Twenty-one squares, totaling 189 square meters, were excavated by hand (Fig. 2). The plowzone, generally extending to a depth of 25 to 30 cm, was excavated as a single unit. Subplowzone excavations proceeded in 10 cm levels but were carried out only in the central portion of the excavations and then only to a depth of 20 or 30 cm below the base of the plowzone. Several one-meter squares were excavated 10 to 20 cm below the plowzone in order to be sure that no further material was to be found. All sediment from the excavations was passed through ¼-inch-mesh screen. Each level from each square was assigned a separate catalog number. This number was used for all specimens from that unit with the exception of certain "special finds," which were plotted *in situ* and assigned separate catalog numbers.

Four additional squares were excavated away from the main block. Two were just off the ridge (Fig. 2); the other two were in a swale to the southeast, about halfway between the existing county road and the main excavation. This latter area was scheduled for alteration by construction of fuel tanks. Excavations in all four squares extended only to the base of the plowzone and produced no cultural material. The sediment was not screened.

On August 8, a backhoe was employed to strip the plowzone from an additional seven units adjacent to the main excavation (Fig. 2). These excavations reached an estimated depth of 20 to 30 cm below the base of the plowzone.

RESULTS

It was suggested in the Introduction that examination of the function of the Airport Site was important for understanding subsistence/settlement systems in the Sangamon River valley and for maximally articulating with the established program of research in this direction. Accordingly, the Airport Site analysis was approached in functional terms in an attempt to understand the nature of activities carried out on the bluff crest of the Sangamon River.

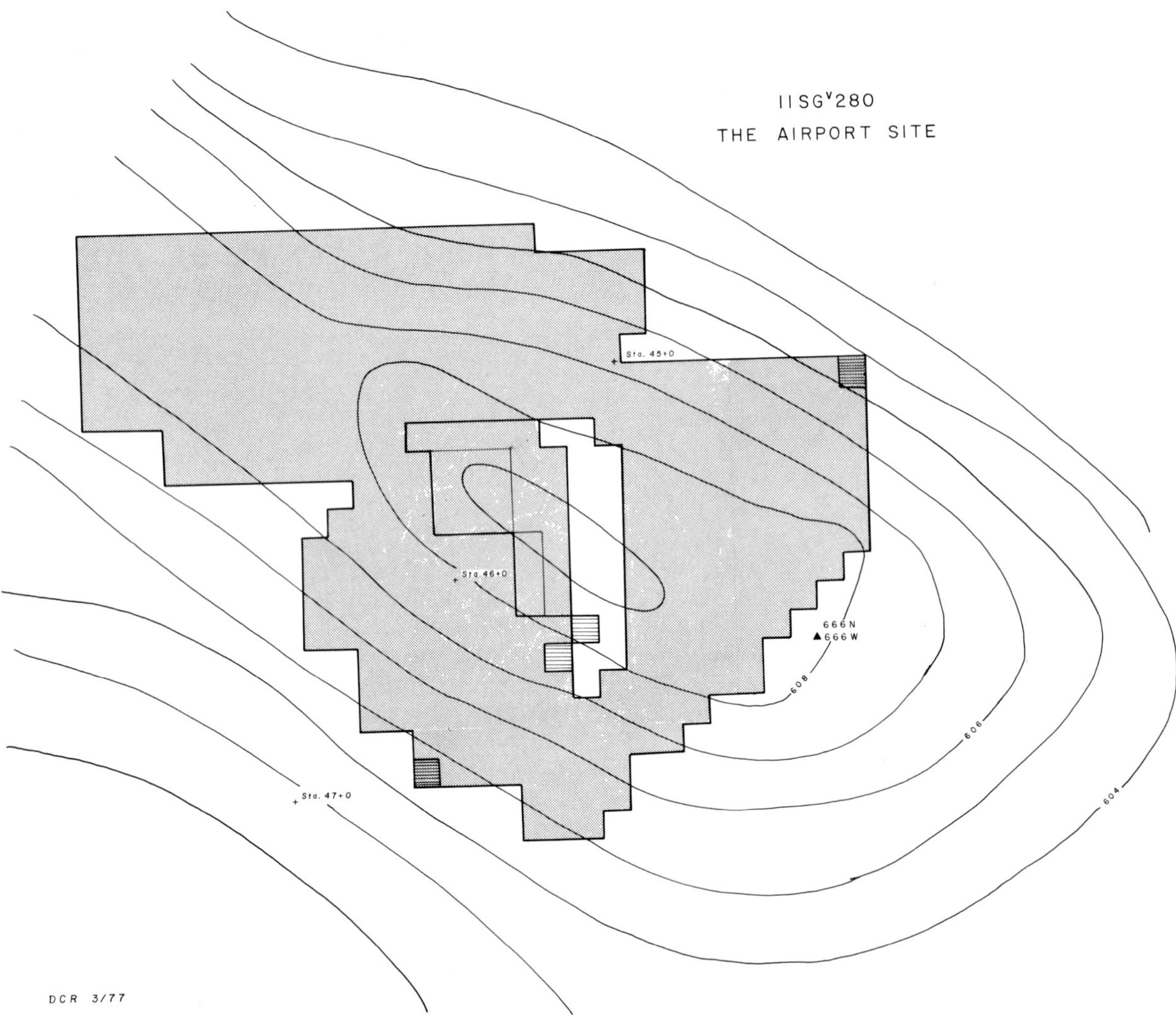

Figure 2. Airport Site: Contour map and plan of investigated area.

ARTIFACTS

A functional classification of artifacts was attempted. Artifacts were grouped on the basis of form with the assumption of a correlation between form and function. Several such classification systems are available in the literature—none of them totally satisfactory but all of them similar in general outline. Since the classification devised by Winters (1969) is one of the better-known schemes available and is a rather standard classification in the Illinois literature, it is employed in the present analysis. Some modification has been introduced in order to account for ceramics and certain unmodified lithic debris. Winters' classification, with additions, is presented in Table 1.

GENERAL UTILITY TOOLS

General utility tools are described by Winters (1969:32) as "tools of such generalized nature that they could have been used in connection with a variety of activities." Basic attributes, including provenience, are given in Table 2.

Knives—2 specimens (Pl. 2,a-b)

Raw Material: Light grey chert.

Form and Technology: The identification of these items as "knives" is based on formal criteria used by Winters (1969:32): "Knives were usually fashioned by removing a series of alternate flakes from adjacent faces of a flake, thus producing a wavy, sawlike edge." Both are triangular artifacts. One (Pl. 2,a) has rounded cor-

4

ners, an excurvate base, and straight lateral margins. The other (Pl. 2,b) has a straight base and irregularly straight margins.

Temporal Affiliation: These specimens resemble the "triangular knives" described for the Riverton Culture in the Wabash Valley (Winters 1969:32). This identification would assign them a Late Archaic temporal provenience.

Scrapers—10 specimens.

CLASS A—Hafted scrapers—2 specimens (Pl. 2,c-d).

Raw Material: Off-white, probably glacial, chert.

Form and Technology: Both scrapers are made from reworked projectile points. One (Pl. 2,c) is on a side-notched point with a ground straight base. The working edge is immediately above the notches, straight, and perpendicular to the lateral margins. The other scraper (Pl. 2,d) is made from a reworked Snyders group point. It has broad parabolic notches, straight base, and a highly convex working edge joining the lateral margins just above the notches. Microscope examination shows rounding and polishing the full length of the working edges of both tools. Judge (1973:154) refers to this kind of wear as "soft" wear, produced by scraping or softening hides. Wilmsen (1970:74) similarly concludes that this type of wear was produced by hide-working.

CLASS B—Flake scrapers—8 specimens (Pl. 2,e-h).

Raw Material: Variable; probably glacial cherts.
Form and Technology: All eight scrapers are made on the ends of flakes, and all are broken. All are unifacial implements, with convex working edges, and are end/side scraper combinations. All working edges are steeply retouched. Microscopically, only one specimen exhibits the same soft wear as the hafted scrapers. No wear was observed at low power (10×) on the other seven scrapers. This lack of wear may indicate a different function or perhaps that these tools were not used long enough to produce wear patterns visible under low power (cf. Brose 1975).

Retouched and/or Utilized Flakes—

11 specimens.

Winters does not include utilized flakes in his classification. They are included here with general utility tools under the assumption that their primary use would be for casual cutting and scraping. The debitage from the Airport Site does not show much incidental use. Only 11 flakes with indications of retouch and/or use

TABLE 1
Functional Classification of Artifacts

GENERAL UTILITY TOOLS
  Knives
  Scrapers
  Choppers
  Hammerstones
WEAPONS
  Hunting Implements
    Projectile Points
  Atlatl Weights
  Fishhooks
FABRICATING OR PROCESSING TOOLS
  Flakers
  Drifts
  Perforators
  Sewing Tools
  Microperforators and Drills
  Reamers
  Abraders
DOMESTIC TOOLS
  Manos
  Metates
  Ceramics
WOODWORKING TOOLS
"DIGGING TOOLS"
ORNAMENTS
CEREMONIAL EQUIPMENT
RECREATIONAL EQUIPMENT
BY-PRODUCTS
  Miscellaneous Fragments
  Shatter
  Flakes
    Whole
    Broken
    Bifacial Retouch
  Fire-cracked Rock

Source: Modified from Winters 1969.

were sorted out of the debris from the site. Eight flakes show wear or use along edges parallel to the force axis of the flake. Five of these eight show wear only on one edge—three on the dorsal surface, two on the ventral; the other three have wear on both edges. Of these latter specimens, two show wear on the dorsal face of both edges, the third on alternate edges. Two broken flakes show use, viz., very steep nibbling, on an edge nearly perpendicular to the force axis of the flake. The eleventh flake is a large expanding flake with irregular nibbling on the ventral side of one margin and irregular fracturing on either side of a distal edge broken obliquely (ca. 45°) to the axis of the flake (Pl. 2,m).

WEAPONS

The tools in this category are termed "hunting tools" on the basis of inferred use as projectile points. However, experimental studies by Ahler

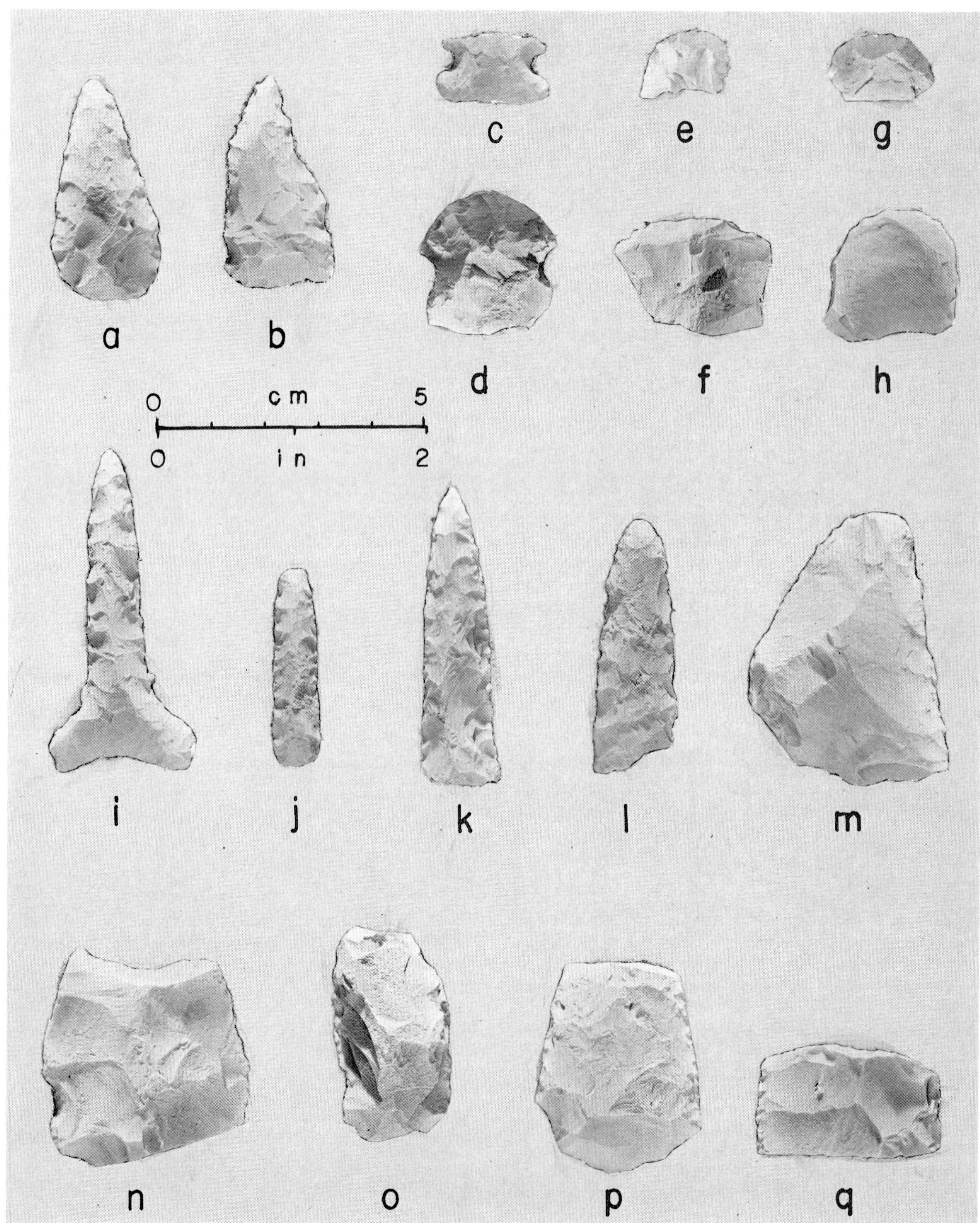

Plate 2. General utility tools, fabricating or processing tools, and by-products.

TABLE 2

Attributes of Knives, Scrapers, and Drills

Class and Specimen	Length	Width	Thickness	Lateral Edge	Base	Weight	Provenience	Illus.
KNIVES								
1	39	20	7	St	Cx	5	684N 702W PZ	Pl. 2,a
2	38	21	7	St	St	7	Surface	Pl. 2,b
SCRAPERS								
A 1	13	21	5	?	St	2	687N 708W PZ	Pl. 2,c
A 2	25	25	9	?	St	5	678N 696W 0–10 BPZ	Pl. 2,d
B 1	30	20	9	?	?	4	684N 699W PZ	
B 2	21	13	9	?	?	2	669N 693W PZ	
B 3	11	20	5	?	?	1	678N 699W PZ	Pl. 2,g
B 4	15	15	6	?	?	1	684N 699W PZ	Pl. 2,e
B 5	21	29	10	?	?	7	705N 696W PZ	Pl. 2,f
B 6	24	25	3	?	?	3	681N 696W PZ	Pl. 2,h
B 7	35	24	7	?	?	6	678N 696W PZ	
B 8	20	28	6	?	?	4	678N 699W PZ	
DRILLS								
A	58	27	8	St	Cc	7	678.81N 696.97W–PZ	Pl. 2,i
B	35	9	6	St	St	2	678N 699W PZ	Pl. 2,j
C 1	50	15	8	St	?	5	683.55N 700.00W 0–10	Pl. 2,k
C 2	42	15	9	Cx	?	5	687N 699W PZ	Pl. 2,l

Note: All measurements are in millimeters.

Lateral Edge and Base:
  Cc—Concave
  Cx—Convex
  St—Straight

PZ—Plow Zone
BPZ—Below Plow Zone

(1971), for example, have shown that they may also have served as cutting tools. In this capacity, they would still have been vital parts of a hunter's tool kit.

Projectile Points—36 specimens.

These points or point parts were found either on the surface of the site or in the excavations. They are grouped into three classes according to their wholeness and the portion of the point represented. They are described here not only as functional indicators but also from a chronological standpoint. Basic attributes, including provenience, are given in Table 3.

CLASS A—Whole points—6 specimens (Pl. 3,a).

Specimen 1.

Raw Material: Grey, probably Dongola, chert.

Form and Technology: It has excurvate lateral margins and a slightly convex base. The haft element is double-notched, i.e., it has side-notches, below which are barbs, below which are corner-notches. The stem is straight-sided with a straight base. The cross section is double-convex or lenticular. It is made on a flake, a portion of the surface remaining on one face.

Temporal Affiliation: Unknown. A similar broken specimen has been collected from the surface of a site elsewhere in Sangamon County.

Specimen 2 (Pl. 3,b).

Raw Material: Light grey chert.

Form and Technology: This point has a triangular blade and broad, shallow corner-notches. The base is convex (and 22-mm-long haft element expands toward the base. The cross section is plano-convex. The whole point is slightly asymmetrical.

Temporal Affiliation: This may be a Steuben Expanding Stemmed point (Morse 1963). The Steuben is a late Middle Woodland and early Late Wodland point, often associated with Weaver ceramics (e.g., Wray and MacNeish 1961; Munson, Parmalee, and Yarnell 1961).

Specimen 3 (Pl. 3,c).

Raw Material: White chert.

Form and Technology: This point has convex lateral margins and a convex base. The haft element is 17 mm long with shallow side-notches. The cross section is plano-convex.

Temporal Affiliation: Unknown.

7

Plate 3. Projectile points and point parts.

Specimen 4 (Pl. 3,e).

Raw Material: White chert.

Form and Technology: This small point has a triangular blade with 90-degree shoulders turning into a straight-sided haft element. The cross section is lenticular. The haft element has a bifurcated base.

Temporal Affiliation: Bifurcated base points are Archaic (cf. J. Chapman, 1975).

Specimen 5 (Pl. 3,d).

Raw Material: White chert.

Form and Technology: The blade element of this small point is triangular with a suggestion of serration. The point has wide parabolic corner-notches with a distinct shoulder. The base is straight. The cross section is double-convex or lenticular.

Temporal Affiliation: The point is probably a Merom Expanding Stemmed point, named by Winters for the Late Archaic period Riverton Culture (1969:151) of the Wabash Valley.

Specimen 6.

Raw Material: Variably colored glacial chert.
Form and Technology: The lateral margins are broadly convex, the base only slightly convex. The point is corner-notched but lack barbs. The cross section is double-convex or lenticular.

CLASS B—Proximal Fragments—
18 specimens.

Group 1—1 specimen (Pl. 3,f).

Raw Material: Variably tan chert.

Form and Technology: Remaining portions of the lateral margins are straight to slightly convex. The small remaining portion of the base is straight. The haft element was probably once corner-notched.
Temporal Affiliation: Unknown.

Group 2—Expanding Stemmed—4 specimens (e.g., Pl. 3,h).

Raw Material: Pinkish to white cherts, probably from glacial deposits.

Form and Technology: All four fragments are from small points, broken below the shoulders. Basal width is 14 to 19 mm. Three specimens have convex bases, the fourth a straight base.

Temporal Affiliation: The size, form, and technology of some of these fragments suggest they are associated with the Late Archaic period Riverton Culture.

Group 3—Side-notched—7 specimens (e.g., Pl. 3,g,i,k).

Raw Materials: All from glacial cherts.

Form and Technology: One specimen is broken through the notches, five are broken mid-blade, and one is obliquely fractured from notch to mid-base. On the five on which blade portions remain, lateral margins are straight. Six of the seven points have straight bases; the other has a slightly convex base. Four have ground bases. One point has impact fracturing nearly splitting it longitudinally from edge to edge. Two other portions of the broken part of the point were recovered from nearby excavation units and fitted to the proximal segment (Pl. 3,g).

Temporal Affiliation: Uncertain.

Group 4—Corner-notched—7 specimens (e.g., Pl. 3,j).

Raw Material: Glacial cherts.

Form and Technology: All are broken above the notches, and all but one are split longitudinally, leaving only one notch. Two have distinct barbs over the notch, the other five appear not to have been barbed.

Temporal Affiliation: Uncertain.

CLASS C —Distal Fragments—12 specimens.

Group 1—1 specimen (Pl. 3,l).

Raw Material: White chert of the Burlington Formation.

Form and Technology: This biface fragment is 52 mm long.

Temporal Affiliation: Could be Late Archaic.

Group 2—Side-notched—1 specimen (Pl. 3,m).

Raw Material: White chert of the Burlington Formation.

Form and Technology: This point is asymmetrically broken, i.e., one side is broken above the notches, the other side is an oblique, slightly curved fracture, probably along an old fracture line in the chert. The blade is a long isosceles triangle. The side-notches are moderately shallow. The cross section is triangular. The point was found in what would have been the throat region of Burial 9 (See Burial 9).

Group 3—8 specimens.

Raw Material: 2 grey Dongola chert; 4 white chert; 2 pink chert.

Form and Technology: These small fragments range from 17 to 24 mm long. Six are snapped at right angles to both surfaces; the other two are broken obliquely through the point.

Group 4—2 specimens (Pl. 3,n-o).

Raw Material: 1 white chert; 1 pink chert.

TABLE 3
Attributes of Projectile Points

Class Specimen		Length	Width	Thickness	Haft	Lateral Edge	Base	Weight	Provenience	Illus.
A	1	44	27	7	DN	Cx	St	20	686.03N 699.20W 0–10	Pl. 3,a
A	2	61	32	11	CN	St	Cx	17	Surface	Pl. 3,b
A	3	48	27	11	CN	Cx	Cx	13	684N 699W PZ	Pl. 3,c
A	4	35	20	6	SM	Cx	Bf	4	672.95N 689.06W Surface	Pl. 3,c
A	5	20	14	6	CN	St	St	1	684N 699W 0–10 BPZ	Pl. 3,d
A	6	30	19	8	CN	Cx	Cx	4	675N 681W Surface	
B1	1	33	29	8	CN	St	St	9	681N 693W PZ	Pl. 3,f
B2	1	9	20	8	ES	?	Cx	1	681N 696W 10–20 BPZ	
B2	2	11	18	5	ES	?	St	1	681N 693W PZ	Pl. 3,h
B2	3	11	14	6	ES	?	Cx	1	678N 699W PZ	
B2	4	12	19	6	ES	?	Cx	2	684N 693W PZ	
B3	1	30	21	8	SN	St	St	8	681N 699W PZ	Pl. 3,g
B3	2	22	20	8	SN	St	St	4	681N 693W PZ	Pl. 3,i
B3	3	24	22	8	SN	St	St	4	687N 696W PZ	
B3	4	20	18	8	SN	St	St	3	681N 696W 10–20 BPZ	
B3	5	12	23	6	SN	?	St	2	675N 693W PZ	
B3	6	26	20	6	SN	St	Cx	4	Surface	Pl. 3,k
B3	7	17	7	7	SN	St	St	1	675N 693W PZ	
B4	1	?	?	6	CN	?	?	1	669N 693W PZ	
B4	2	20	21	8	CN	St	?	4	687N 687W Surface	
B4	3	18	18	4	CN	St	Cx	1	681N 696W 0–10 BPZ	
B4	4	?	?	6	CN	?	?	1	684N 699W 0–10 BPZ	
B4	5	13	18	5	CN	?	Cx	1	684N 693W PZ	Pl. 3,j
B4	6	17	14	7	CN	?	?	2	678N 696W PZ	
B4	7									
C1	1	52	32	10	?	St	?	14	687N 792W PZ	Pl. 3,l
C2	1	48	20	10	SN	St	?	8	681N 696W 10–20 BPZ	Pl. 3,m
C3	1	24	15	3	?	St	?	1	Surface	
C3	2	19	19	5	?	St	?	2	678N 696W PZ	
C3	3	21	17	4	?	Cx	?	1	678N 696W PZ	
C3	4	24	21	7	?	St	?	3	687N 702W PZ	
C3	5	17	15	6	?	Cx	?	1	684N 699W PZ	
C3	6	18	16	7	?	St	?	1	663N 693W PZ	
C3	7	18	16	5	?	St	?	1	678N 699W PZ	
C3	8	14	8	4	?	St	?	1	684N 693W PZ	
C4	1	40	20	8	?	Cx	?	7	681N 693W PZ	Pl. 3,n
C4	2	50	28	9	?	Cx	?	15	681N 696W 10–20 BPZ	Pl. 3,o

Note: All measurements are in millimeters. All weights are in grams.
PZ—Plow Zone
BPZ—Below Plow Zone

Lateral Edge and Base:
  Bf—Bifurcated
  Cc—Concave
  Cx—Convex
  St—Straight

Haft:
  CN—Corner-notched
  DN—Double-notched
  ES—Expanding-stemmed
  SM—Stemmed
  SN—Side-notched

Form and Technology: Two fragments were broken through the notches and, additionally, are missing small tip fragments. Both have very slightly convex lateral margins.

FABRICATING OR PROCESSING TOOLS
Drills—4 specimens.

CLASS A—T-headed drill—1 specimen (Pl. 2,i).
  Raw Material: Grey chert.
  Form and Technology: The shaft of the drill is 45 mm long and straight-sided, widening to 13 mm before flaring out into the T-shaped head. The total length is 58 mm. The head has a maximum width of 27 mm, with a slightly concave base. The cross section of the shaft is diamond-shaped. T-headed drills are usually regarded as having been manufactured by reworking projectile points. The shape of the drill head and the heavy basal grinding suggest that the drill was perhaps made from a reworked Early Archaic Thebes point.

  Temporal Affiliation: Unknown.

CLASS B—Straight Drill—1 specimen (Pl. 2,j).
Raw Material: White to light tan chert.

Form and Technology: The sides of this 38-mm-long drill are straight and nearly parallel to one another. The tip is 6 mm wide, the base 9 mm wide. The cross section is diamond-shaped and 6 mm thick. The tool would doubtless have been ineffective for piercing but could have served as a reamer for an already-started hole. Microscopic examination, however, revealed no clear use marks to support or refute this notion.
Temporal Affiliation: Unknown.

CLASS C—Broken Drills—2 specimens
(Pl. 2,k-l).
Raw Material: White chert.

Form and Technology: Only the shafts of these drills remain. One (Pl. 2,k) is 50 mm long, 15 mm wide, and 8 mm thick. It has straight sides. The other (Pl. 2,l) is 42 mm long, 15 mm wide, 9 mm thick, and has slightly convex lateral margins. Bases are missing on both specimens. The first drill has a diamond-shaped cross section, the second, a fat biconvex shape.
Temporal Affiliation: Unknown.

DOMESTIC TOOLS

Items included under this heading would presumably function in such household activities as food preparation and consumption.

Manos—4 specimens (Pl. 4,g).
Raw Material: 2 of rhyolite, 1 of basalt, 1 of sandstone.

Form and Technology: Oblong, hand-size rocks, ground flat on both sides. One rhyolite mano shows shallow pitting on both sides. All specimens have been plow-damaged.
Temporal Affiliation: Unknown.

Ceramics

A total of 29 sherds were recovered. Unfortunately, most are small and the total includes only three rims, two of which are quite small. The pottery is divided into two categories, representing two or at most three vessels.

CATEGORY A—18 sherds—1 rim, 17 body
(Pl. 4,a).
Paste and Temper: Fine compact paste; abundant quantities of black, angular, grit temper. Temper particles range up to 4 mm in maximum dimension.

Thickness: 4 to 7 mm.

Color: Tan to reddish tan. The color is reasonably uniform throughout the sherd, i.e., no distinct firing core appears.

External Surface Treatment: Several sherds are cord-marked. Cord impressions are deep and parallel to one another. The other sherds have eroded or spalled surfaces, making it impossible to judge surface treatment. Surfaces on the cord-marked sherds are not well-enough preserved to determine cord-twist detail.

Rim: The single rim sherd is small. Its description in general follows that above. Additionally, it is three mm thick at the lip which is flattened and perpendicular to the interior and exterior surfaces. The profile tapers toward the lip and is very slightly curved.

Decoration: Only the rim sherd is decorated. Decoration consists of hemiconical punctates on the exterior surface directly below the lip. The punctates are 5 mm long, 3 mm wide, spaced 3 mm apart, and at a slight angle to the lip. They are placed over a smoothed surface.

Temporal Affiliation: Identification of this vessel is somewhat uncertain; however, paste, temper, thickness, etc., all correspond to the published descriptions of Weaver Ware (cf. Wray and MacNeish 1961:52). Additionally, the single row of hemiconical punctates below the lip is characteristic of Weaver Plain, var. Plain Stamped (Griffin 1952:121).

CATEGORY B—11 sherds—2 rim, 9 body
(Pl. 4,b-e).
Paste and Temper: Fine sandy paste, not as well consolidated as vessel A; abundant white grit temper. At least two sherds have chert particles included in the temper. Individual temper particles range up to 6 mm in maximum dimension.

Color: Variable, exterior surface is light brown to brownish-orange; interior surface is same as exterior to black; core is reddish-orange on some sherds, even color throughout on others.

External Surface Treatment: Smoothed or smoothed-over cord-marked. Cord impressions are not clear enough to discern cord-twist.

Rim: Two rim sherds, almost certainly from the same vessel, are included among the collections from the site. The sherds are 2 to 12 mm thick at the lip which is flattened and perpendicular to both surfaces. The external surface is cord-marked up to 15 mm from the lip on the larger of the two pieces. The upper 15 mm is smoothed, with the wiping lines parallel to the lip. The profile shows a pronounced curve and a trace of thickening at the lip (Pl. 4,b).

Decoration: Confined to the rim sherds. The interior of the vessel is decorated with cord-wrapped-stick impressions directly below the lip. Impressions are 15 to 18 mm long, 1.1 mm wide,

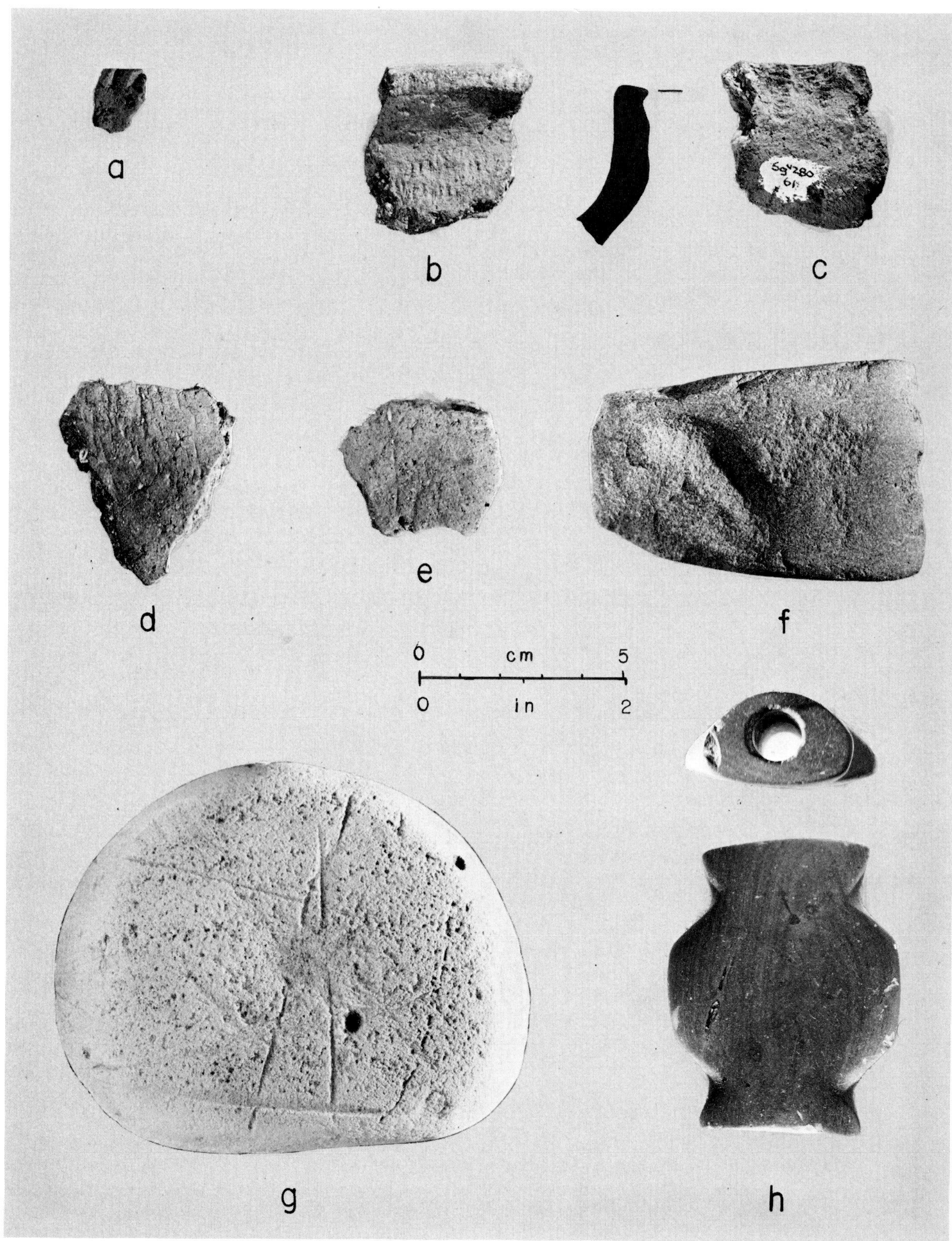

Plate 4. Domestic items and ceremonial equipment.

TABLE 4

Attributes of Mortuary Bifaces

Class and Specimen	Length	Width	Thickness	Haft	Lateral Edge	Base	Weight	Length/ Width	Length/ Thickness	Provenience
A a	223	43	12	L	Re	Cc	129	5.2	18.6	Surface
A b	222	44	13	L	Re	Cc	122	5.0	17.1	Sur. & 684N 696W
A c	187	44	10	L	Re	Cc	89	4.3	18.7	Sur. & 684N 696W
B a	213	45	19	L	Cx	St	188	4.7	11.2	688.23N 698.70W
B b	191	51	19	L	Re	St	194	3.7	10.1	680.70N 701.60W
B c	139*	47	10	L	Ex	Cc	82*	3.0	13.9	684N 693W PZ & 678N 696W PZ
C a	179	24	9	L	Cx	Cx	45	7.5	19.9	683.15N 697.47W 0–10
C b	199	30	12	L	Cx	Cx	62	6.6	16.6	686.03N 699.82W 0–10
D a	177	34	12	L	Cx	St	72	5.2	14.8	Surface
D b	261	46	24	L	Cx	St	260	5.7	10.9	680.55N 695.90W Sur.
E 1	192	37	15	CN	Cx	St	95	5.2	12.8	687N 696W PZ & 687N 699W PZ 687N 699W PZ
E 2	240	51	13	BN	Re	St	119	4.7	18.5	681N 696W PZ
E 3	177	39	11	SN	Cx	St	91	4.5	16.1	679.47N 699.00W PZ

* Incomplete specimen.

Note: All measurements are in millimeters. All weights are in grams.

PZ—Plow Zone
BPZ—Below Plow Zone

Lateral Edge and Base:	Haft:
Cc—Concave	BN—Basally Notched
Cx—Convex	CN—Corner-notched
Ex—Excurvate	L—Lanceolate
Re—Recurvate	SN—Side-notched
St—Straight	

2.5 mm deep, and are spaced 2 to 4 mm apart. Fragments of charred material adhere to the cord-wrapped-stick impressions.

Temporal Affiliation: Paste and temper characteristics suggest Havana Ware. Cord-wrapped-stick impressions are common on Havana Ware vessels but are rarely found on the interior of Havana rims from central Illinois. They do, however, occur on the interior of local Havana types (variants) in southwestern Wisconsin (Hurley 1974, Wittry 1959). Thus, although identification of the Airport Site sherds is uncertain, it is suggested that they are from a Havana vessel.

CEREMONIAL EQUIPMENT

Items in this category could perhaps be placed under other headings but are grouped here because of spatial proximity to the burials and similarity to items in mortuary assemblages elsewhere in the Midwest.

Large Chipped Stone Bifaces—13 specimens.

These pieces are differentiated from the remainder of the chipped stone assemblage by their size, form, technology, and lack of evidence of use. They display a surprisingly wide range of variation in morphology and technology. The following division is based in part upon general proportions of the artifacts, as graphed in Figure 3, crosscut by variation in morphology and technology. Basic attributes, including provenience, are given in Table 4.

CLASS A—3 specimens (Pl. 5,a-c).

Raw Material: White chert of the Burlington Formation.

Form: These are slender, recurvate-edged lanceolate bifaces, flared at the proximal end. The base is straight to very slightly concave. Length/width ratios range from 4.3 to 5.2, length/thickness ratios from 17.1 to 18.7. All three artifacts have lenticular cross sections.

Technology: Flake scars on all surfaces show flat, expanding flakes with prominent ripples. The edges show narrow parallel flaking extending about 7 mm onto the surface.

Temporal Affiliation: These are identified as Wadlow points. The name was given by Perino (1968:98) and has been used by Houart (1971:31) and Cook (n.d.:50) to designate the diagnostic artifact form for Horizon IV at the Koster Site in Greene County, Illinois. Titterington

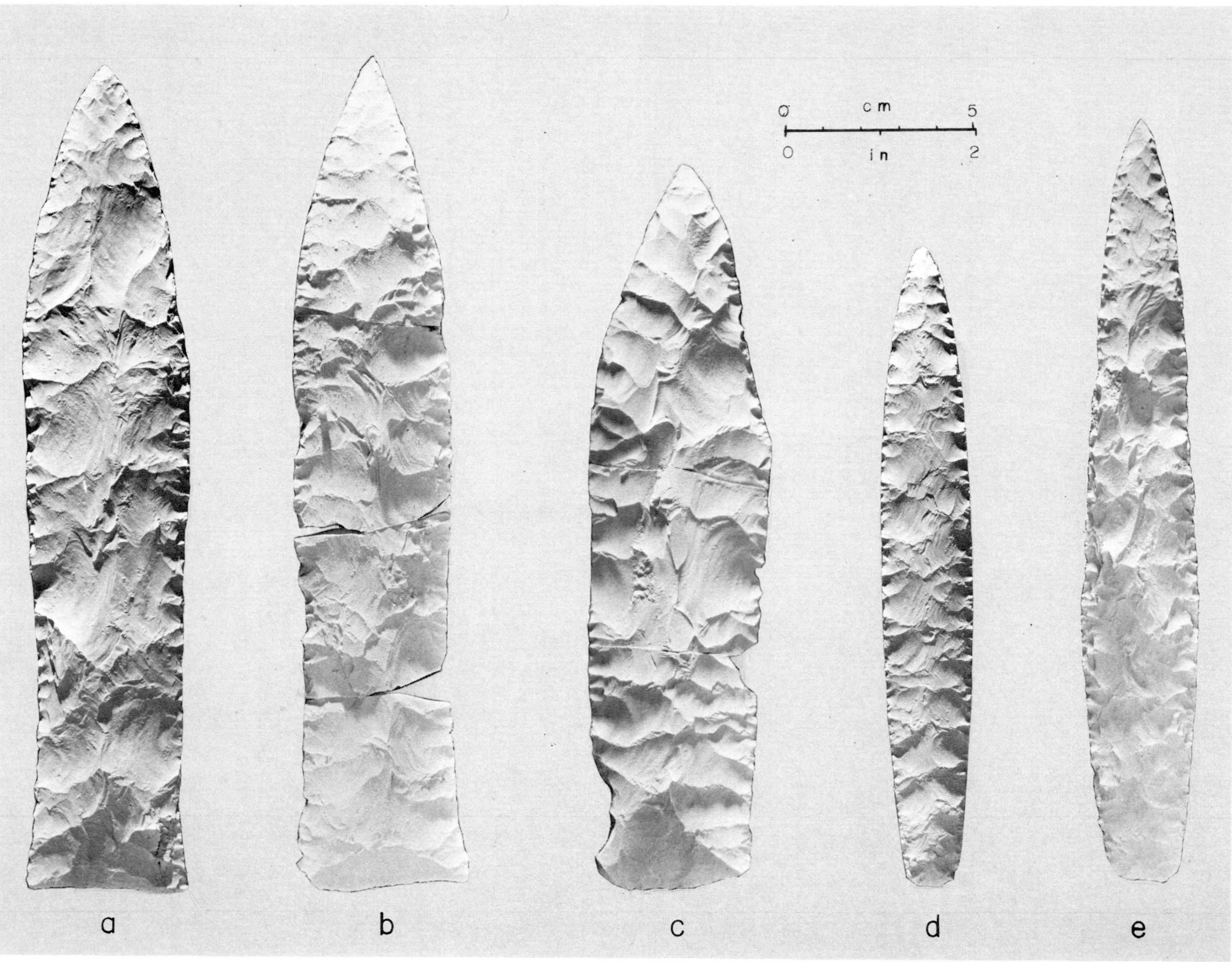

Plate 5.   Large chipped stone bifaces.

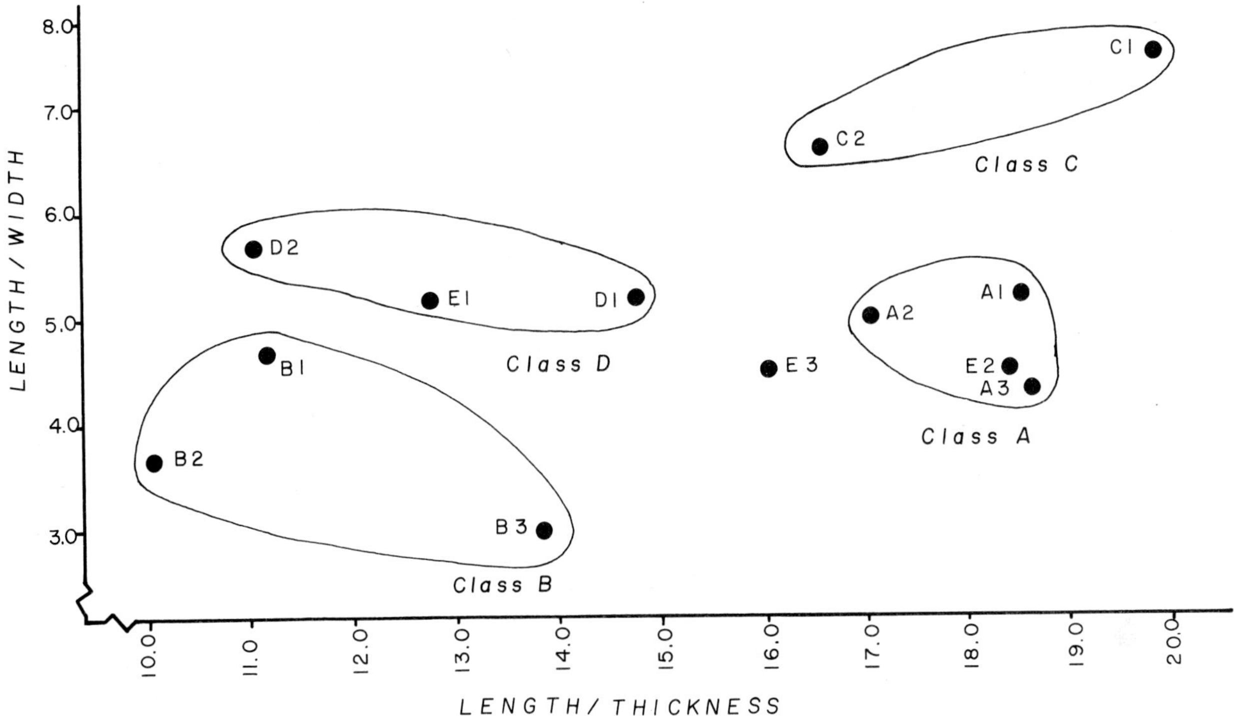

Figure 3. Proportions of large chipped stone bifaces, classes A through E (Ceremonial Equipment). Horizontal axis shows the length/thickness ratio; vertical axis shows the length/width ratio (see Table 4).

(1950) refers to these as "Type 2" points at a series of mortuary sites in the St. Louis area. At these sites, Wadlow points occur in large numbers. They are generally associated with the Late Archaic period.

CLASS B—3 specimens (Pl. 6,a-c).

Raw Material: White chert of the Burlington Formation.

Form: Slightly recurvate edges, with less-pronounced flaring at the base than on the Class A specimens. The base is straight to slightly convex. Length/width ratios are 3.0 to 4.7; length/thickness ratios 10.1 to 13.9 (Fig. 3). In other words, these points are somewhat shorter in relation to width and considerably thicker in relation to length than are the Class A specimens. Cross sections are all double-convex.

Technology: Flake scars reflect flat, primary flaking with expanding, prominently rippled flakes. There is some fine working along the edges. One specimen shows a gloss on both surfaces, probably on the original chert blank rather than wear on the present artifact.

Temporal Affiliation: Same as Class A.

CLASS C—2 specimens (Pl. 5,d-e).

Raw Material: White chert of the Burlington Formation.

Form: These are long, narrow bifaces with slightly convex lateral margins and straight bases. Length/width ratios are 6.6 to 7.5 length/thickness ratios are 16.6 to 16.9, making them similarly length/width-proportioned but thinner in relation to length than the Class A artifacts (Fig. 3). Both specimens have lenticular cross sections.

Technology: Both pieces show fine parallel secondary working along the edges, producing an even margin. One specimen has lateral grinding on the lower 52 mm of the lateral margins.

Temporal Affiliation: Probably Late Archaic. Lanceolate bifaces similar to these were found with Wadlow points in Koster Horizon IV (Houart 1971:32, Cook n.d.:53) and at the Late Archaic Booth (Klippel 1969) and Hunt (Klippel n.d.) sites in Missouri. They are also similar to Sedalia and Nebo Hill points from western Missouri (C. Chapman 1975).

CLASS D—2 specimens (Pl. 6,d-e).

Raw Material: White chert of the Burlington Formation.

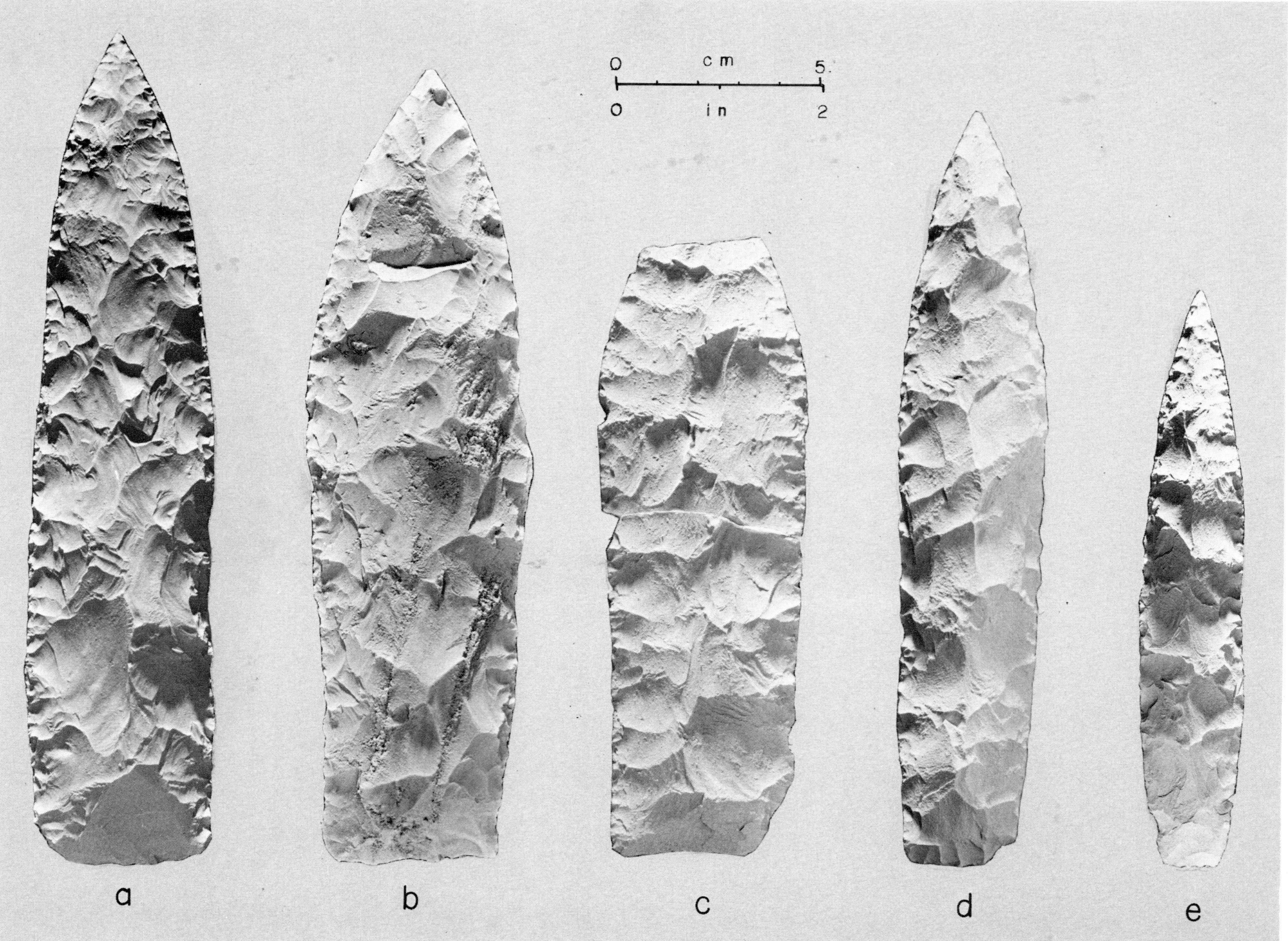

Plate 6. Large chipped stone bifaces.

Form: These are lanceolate bifaces with slightly convex lateral margins and straight bases. One specimen has a double triangular cross section, the other is plano-triangular. Length/width ratios are 5.2 to 5.7 while length/thickness ratios are 10.9 to 14.8. These specimens are thus similarly length/width-proportioned to those in Class B but thinner in relation to length.

Technology: The major feature differentiating this class technologically from Class C is the lack of fine secondary flaking and the lack of either basal or lateral grinding. Lateral margins are thus irregular, and there is a pronounced longitudinal ridge, reflected in the cross-section descriptions.

Temporal Affiliation: Same as Class C.

CLASS E—3 specimens.
Specimen 1—(Pl. 7,a).

Raw Material: White chert of the Burlington Formation.

Form: This biface is a hafted equivalent of Class D. The length/width ratio of 5.2 and length/thickness of 12.8 both fall squarely within the ranges of the specimens in that class (Fig. 3). The difference is the presence on this specimen of shallow, hyperbolic corner-notches, giving rise to weak shoulders and a slightly expanding stem. The base of the haft element is straight. The irregular cross section is triangular.

Technology: Similar in most respects to Class C. An irregularly thick surface suggests that the maker had some trouble thinning the specimen. Some secondary working is apparent on the blade.

Temporal Affiliation: Late Archaic. Klippel (1969:10) discusses similar specimens from the Booth Site in Missouri.

Specimen 2—(Pl. 7,b).

Raw Material: White chert of the Burlington Formation.

Form: Similar to a hafted version of Class A, this point has recurvate margins and flares widely at the base. The length/width ratio of 4.7 and length/thickness ratio of 18.5 fall into the range of specimens in Class A. The cross section is lenticular. The point is basally notched with 18 mm deep parabolic notches and long barbs. The stem is straight-sided and straight-based.

Technology: Similar to Class A.

Temporal Affiliation: Late Archaic. This point is an example of what Scully (1951:2) has named the "Etley" point. It was also found by Titterington (1950) at his nonpottery sites near St. Louis and is considered a diagnostic artifact of the Titterington phase. Etley points were found with Wadlow points at the Booth (Klippel 1969) and Hunt (Klippel n.d.) sites in Missouri and the

Koster Site in Illinois (Cook n.d.). C. Chapman (1975:257) has named the square-based variant of the Etley, such as the present specimen, the Stone Square Stemmed.

Specimen 3—(Pl. 7,c).

Raw Material: Speckled green chert with small red spots. Texturally, this material is similar to Mill Creek chert but is of a color never reported for Mill Creek. The provenience of this chert is unknown.

Form: This point has nearly parallel sides, curving to a point at the distal end, and a straight base. It is side-notched. The length/width ratio is 4.5; length/thickness ratio is 16.1. Side-notches are 11 to 12 mm wide, and 3 to 6 mm deep, terminating about 12 mm above the base-lateral margin juncture. The upper portion of the blade element has a pronounced counter-clockwise twist. The blade has a lenticular cross section.

Technology: Flat, expanding flakes. The fine parallel flaking on both edges of both faces produces very even lateral margins.

Temporal Affiliation: Probably Late Archaic, the identification of this point is less certain than for the other specimens. It is not unlike the Hemphill Notched (Scully 1951:7), also found in Titterington sites near St. Louis (Titterington 1950), and other Late Archaic forms in the Great Lakes area, such as the Osceola Point (Ritzenthaler 1946:63).

Bannerstone—1 specimen (Pl. 4,h).

Raw Material: Banded ferruginous siltstone.

Size: 66 mm long, 54 mm wide, 24 mm thick; the bore hole is circular and 12 mm in diameter. The flared end is 37 mm wide but 33 mm wide in the constricted neck. Weight = 114 gm.

Form: This is an example of the "Single-Face Bottle" bannerstone type of Knoblock (1939: 297–302). It is roughly rectangular with constrictions, like bottlenecks, at either end, flaring out to ends somewhat narrower than the maximum width of the whole specimen. The cross section is plano-convex. Some breakage occurs on the planar face. This may not be postdepositional breakage, however. Webb (1974:328) discussed the possibility of purposeful breakage, or "killing" of bannerstones before interment at the Indian Knoll Site in Kentucky. Whether the Airport Site specimen was "killed" is not known, but the break does not appear to be recent, and the missing piece was not found.

Temporal Affiliation: Bannerstones are frequently considered diagnostic of the Late Archaic period. They were abundant at the Indian Knoll

Plate 7. Large chipped stone bifaces.

(Webb 1974) and Ferry (Fowler 1957) sites, both Late Archaic, as well as occurring at five of Titterington's (1950) nonpottery mortuary sites in the St. Louis area.

Celts—2 specimens.
Specimen 1 (Pl. 4,f).
   Raw Material: Grey diorite.
   Size: 80 mm long, 49 mm wide at the bit, 32 mm wide at the poll. Maximum width is 51 mm just behind the bit. Maximum thickness is 11 mm at the poll, tapering evenly to the bit.
   Form: Basically in the shape of an elongated trapezoid. The cross section at the poll is rectangular; the longitudinal section is wedge-shaped. The posterior half of the artifact appears to have a clockwise twist, which may, however, be the result of very heavy battering. The bit also shows some damage. The surface (where not damaged) is smoothly polished.

Specimen 2.
   Raw Material: Sandstone concretion
   Size: 410 mm long; 73 mm wide at the bit, 38 mm wide at the poll; 37 mm thick at the bit, 46 mm thick at the poll. The weight is greater than 2600 grams.
   Form: This long, narrow celt was made by rounding the ends of a natural sandstone concretion. One end is only slightly wider than the other. The cross section and longitudinal section are both rectangular with rounded corners.
   Temporal Affiliation: To this writer's knowledge, such an artifact is unreported in the Illinois literature. However, its clear association with a presumably Late Archaic burial (see Burial 9) suggests a Late Archaic temporal provenience at the Airport Site. A stone celt did occur at one of Titterington's sites (1950).

By-products
   These are categories of waste products from activities that occurred at the site and are almost certainly primary refuse, i.e., refuse discarded at its location of use (Schiffer 1972:161).

Miscellaneous Bifacial Fragments—
32 specimens—(e.g., Pl. 2,n-q).
   All of these pieces are bifacially worked fragments from broken artifacts. By themselves, they are not identifiable to class and are therefore placed in a miscellaneous category.

Unmodified Debitage—1761 pieces
   Unmodified chert debitage is presumed to result from manufacture or maintenance of chipped stone tools. The flakes were not otherwise modified, nor is evidence of incidental use apparent.

Unmodified debitage has been sorted into four classes:

Class 1: Shatter—Blocky, angular fragments of stone with no bulbs of percussion, presumably by-products of the flintknapping process.

Class 2: Flakes with striking platforms and bulbs of percussion—removed during manufacture of stone tools.

Class 3: Broken flakes (possibly broken flakes from Class 2)—thin and rippled on the ventral surface but broken and lacking striking platforms or bulbs of percussion.

Class 4: Flakes from bifacial retouching or resharpening (a subset of Class 2) distinguished by a wide, faceted, lipped striking platform, retaining a portion of the former edge of the tool, presumably by-products of manufacture or maintenance of bifacial tools (cf. Frison 1968; Vehik 1974).

   Provenience information is given in Table 5.

Fire-cracked Rock and Sandstone

   A total of 181,238 grams (181.238 kilograms) of miscellaneous pieces of rock and sandstone were collected from the excavations.

BONE

Human
   Fragments of human bone were profuse on the surface and/or in the plowzone of approximately a 60-m^2 area. More substantial bone fragments, although still shallow and poorly preserved, were encountered at the base of the plowzone and at depths of about 50 cm below the surface. At least 13 burials, this count based on skulls or major skull fragments, were represented. Other elements included mostly long bones, the identification of which was made difficult by the lack of ends on most shafts. Grave or pit features were not observed, even with the deepest burials. Such features, if present, should have been readily discernible in the light yellow subsoil. The descriptions following are therefore somewhat tenuous. The distribution of major skeletal elements excavated is shown in Figure 4; burial characteristics are summarized in Table 6. In the following discussion, skeletal terminology follows that of Bass (1971).
Burial 1—A portion of a calvarium was accompanied by partial shafts of three long bones. The skull part was about 0.2 m due west of the long bones. Two long bones were crossed at a highly acute angle; the third paralleled the top bone about 0.05 m to the west. Orientation of the long bones was generally slightly west of north.

TABLE 5

Debitage Summary

Provenience	Class				Size-Grade	
	1	2	3	4	½″	¼″
666N 690W PZ	6	5	2	1	1	12
663N 693W PZ	2	8	6	0	3	16
663N 693W 0–10 BPZ	1	2	1	0	1	4
678N 693W PZ	27	12	19	1	14	42
681N 693W PZ	56	35	18	1	15	90
675N 693W PZ	9	36	18	1	10	57
684N 693W PZ	42	40	23	0	10	93
672N 693W PZ	22	13	19	0	7	50
683N 695W 0–10 BPZ	1	0	0	0	1	1
684N 695W 0–10 BPZ	1	2	0	0	0	3
669N 693W PZ	28	16	24	0	10	64
651N 708W PZ	0	0	0	0	0	0
693N 660W PZ	0	0	0	0	0	0
684N 696W PZ	34	26	29	1	5	76
681N 696W PZ	46	33	28	3	18	84
678N 696W PZ	29	17	16	6	8	69
687N 696W PZ	24	34	29	1	8	81
686N 698W 0–10 BPZ	0	6	1	0	1	6
684N 699W PZ	41	32	34	5	10	103
678N 696W 0–10 BPZ	13	10	14	1	6	34
684N 699W 0–10 BPZ	9	10	9	0	5	25
687N 699W PZ	30	22	22	1	13	69
678N 699W PZ	24	18	19	1	4	60
678N 699W 0–10 BPZ	24	8	7	0	12	27
678N 699W 10–20 BPZ	13	10	6	2	6	27
681N 699W PZ	34	22	26	1	5	81
681N 699W 0–10 BPZ	17	7	15	2	3	38
681N 699W 10–20 BPZ	11	9	8	1	5	25
684N 702W PZ	10	16	19	2	11	38
687N 702W PZ	24	35	9	0	7	61
687N 705W PZ	32	20	16	0	12	60
681N 696W 0–10 BPZ	9	9	4	1	1	22
684N 705W PZ	22	19	15	1	11	48
681N 696W 10–20 BPZ	15	13	9	0	2	38
681N 694.5W 0–10 BPZ	9	2	9	0	1	19
687N 708W PZ	11	11	20	0	7	35

PZ—Plow Zone
BPZ—Below Plow Zone

TABLE 6

Burial Summary

Skull	Mode of Interment	Orientation*	Direction Facing	Provenience
1	Bundle	W–E	?	681N693W
2	Bundle	?	NW	681N696W
3	Bundle	W–E	N or NW	681N696W
4	Bundle	?	E?	681N696W
5	Bundle	?	?	681N696W
6	Bundle	SE–NW	E	681N696W
7	Bundle?	SE–NW	E	681N696W
8	Bundle	NE–SW	E	681N696W
9	Extended	NW–SE	?	681N696W
10	Bundle	?	NW	678N696W
11	Bundle	S–N	S	684N699W
12	Bundle	SW–NE	?	684N699W
13	Bundle	?	?	678N699W

* Head to foot.

Figure 4. Distribution of major skeletal remains.

Burial 2—The skull, labeled No. 2, was one of three found in close proximity to one another, at the same level, and scattered among a number of long bone fragments. Skull 2 was 0.9 m due west of, and at the same level as, the skull from Burial 1. Determining which long bones go with which skulls is difficult. Only a crushed portion of the calvarium of Skull 2 remained. It appeared to have been resting on the parietals. Since portions of the occipital were present to the southeast, the skull was apparently facing northwest. One long-bone shaft was in contact with the underside of the skull. Portions of six other long bones were recorded nearby, four of these with the same general northwest-southeast orientation as the bone tangential to the skull, the other two at nearly right angles (i.e., northeast-southwest). The Etley point (Class E, Spec. 2, Pl. 7,b) lay approximately 0.3 m southeast of and at the same level as the skull. Like the long bones, it was oriented in a northwest-southeast direction with its base to the southeast.

Burial 3—This calvarium lay 0.7 m northwest of the skull from Burial 2 and about 0.45 m

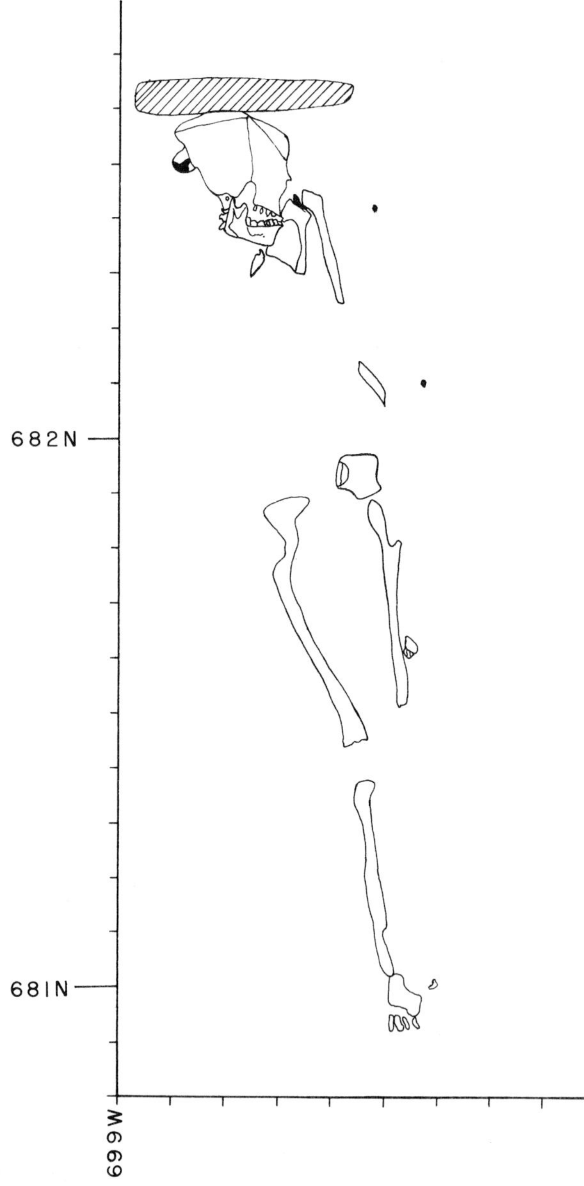

Figure 5. Burial 9. Note sandstone celt (Ceremonial Equipment, Celts, Specimen 2) directly above skull, and projectile point (Weapons, Class C, Specimen 2) in throat region. All other items shown are bone fragments.

north of Burial 4. Immediately to the east of Skull 3 was a stack of long bones piled parallel to one another and oriented east-west. At least 10 bones were present, some of which may represent long bones associated with another skull. The cranium was only partially intact; it probably faced north or northwest. Several teeth were scattered nearby.

Burial 4—This skull was 0.45 m south of Skull 3, and 0.3 m west of Skull 2. Other than a shaft section, 0.1 m long, sitting atop the skull, no long bones were obviously associated with this skull. The cranium itself was crushed flat. It appears, however, to have faced east. A portion of the mandible and several teeth lay immediately to the east.

Burial 5—This fragmentary skull section lay 0.65 m southeast of Skull 4, 0.5 m southwest of Skull 5, and on the same level as both of these skulls. Its orientation is impossible to determine due to its very fragmentary state of preservation. Although no long bones can be definitely assigned to this burial, this skull was only about 0.2 m south of one of the shafts mentioned with Burial 2.

Burial 6—This fairly complete cranium with associated long bones was buried slightly deeper than the previously described skulls, was less adversely affected by the plow, and therefore is somewhat more describable. The skull is probably that of an adult male whose age at death was not determinable in the field. It lay on its right side, facing east. Neither any portion of the mandible nor any of the teeth remained. Two long-bone shaft fragments were underneath the skull; three others, apparently from an arm still articulated at time of interment, leaned against the skull. At least eight other long-bone parts were scattered with a north-south orientation to the east and northeast of the skull and at depths equal to or slightly above the level of Skull 6, but below Skulls 2 and 5.

Burial 7—This skull lay 0.8 m southwest of Burial 3, 0.8 m northwest of Skull 4, and 0.65 m northeast of Skull 8. Although damaged by plow action, the skull appeared to be facing east. A mandible fragment was articulated with a portion of the maxilla, both wth several teeth remaining. Heavy dental attrition indicates probable middle age for the individual at time of death. No other bones were clearly associated with this skull. However, a scatter of long-bone shafts and bone scraps lay 0.55 m to the north of this skull. Since these latter bone fragments were not accompanied by a skull fragment, they may belong to Burial 7. This therefore *could* have been the remains of an extended burial. The general orientation of the bone scatter, including the skull, is northwest-southeast. One large biface was found on the surface above the long-bone scatter; two fragments of another biface were found higher in the plowzone above this same bone scatter.

Burial 8—This damaged calvarium lay amidst a scatter of long-bone shaft sections. Although the individual bones were oriented generally northwest-southeast, the overall configuration was northeast-southwest. One point (Class C,

Spec. a) was found oriented also northwest-southeast directly below a bone-shaft fragment. The skull was resting on the calvarium, with the foramen magnum up and the occipital region to the west.

Burial 9—This burial was the deepest and best preserved at the Airport Site. It is that of a male estimated to have died in his early twenties, using criteria discussed by Bass (1971). The skeleton was extended in a supine position and was undoubtedly primary. Although it was the most complete burial encountered, only the cracked skull, several cervical vertebrae, portions of the left arm, pelvis fragments, both femora, the right tibia, and portions of the right foot remained (Fig. 5). Two left ossicles (malleus and incus) were also preserved and were found while cleaning the skull in the laboratory. A single projectile point (Class C, Spec. 2) was found in the throat region (Fig. 5). A large sandstone celt, described above, rested directly above and slightly under the head. The burial was oriented slightly west of north-south, with the head to the north and facing east.

Burial 10—Only part of the calvarium of the skull remained. Orientation is impossible to determine. This skull was isolated at the southern edge of the bone scatter. It was 3.55 m south and slightly west of Skull 5 and 2.1 m southeast of Skull 13. No other bones were clearly associated with this skull, although a number of long-bone sections occurred in the space between this skull and that of Burial 5.

Burials 11 and 12—These two consisted of skull parts piled with a number of long-bone sections and other bone fragments in the northwestern corner of the bone scatter. The skull for Burial 11 was 0.6 m northeast of Burial 12. The general orientation of the bone scatter was northeast-southwest.

Burial 13—This very fragmentary skull section was accompanied by a number of poorly preserved fragments of the postcranial skeleton. Details and orientation are impossible to determine. The skull is 2.1 m northwest of Burial 10, and 2.4 m southwest of Burial 8.

Nonhuman Bone

Only 8 nonhuman bone elements were collected. Two of these, including one snake vertebra, were undoubtedly recent intrusions. Three are tooth fragments: one from a beaver incisor, two from deer molars. One small fragment of turtle carapace and two small unidentifiable scraps of bone comprise the remainder of the nonhuman bone assemblage. All elements were from either the plowzone or the surface.

RECENT DETRITUS

Although the Airport Site shows little historic disturbance other than agricultural activity, it lay between an automobile junkyard and a county road. Not surprisingly, therefore, a small quantity of historic refuse was encountered. This was all in the plowzone and consisted mostly of nails and glass.

DISCUSSION

Two distinct functions and three temporally separate ocupations may be recognized at the Airport Site. The two obvious functions are those of a mortuary site or cemetery and a hunting camp. In probable order, the three occupations are those by the Late Archaic Titterington Phase, Late Archaic Riverton Culture, and the Middle-Late Woodland peoples.

TITTERINGTON FOCUS

The mortuary function of the site is indeed its most prominent feature. At least thirteen burials, poorly preserved, were laid out in a roughly oblong area about 9 m northwest-southeast by 6 m northeast-southwest, corresponding with the highest part of the sand ridge (Figs. 1 and 2). One skeleton was extended in a supine position; the other 12 were probably bundle burials. The burial procedure apparently entailed stacking long bones near skulls.

In inferred mortuary association were 13 large chipped stone bifaces—already identified as relating to the Late Archaic Titterington Focus—two celts, and one bannerstone. Figure 6 plots the distributions of these artifacts in relation to skulls or skull fragments. Most of the small group of artifacts to the north of the burials consists of fragments of bifaces rather than complete specimens. The present tenant stated that he had always plowed the field in a north-south direction. Thus, although plow-drag at the Airport Site has been minimal (Roper 1976), it may have resulted in the displacement of the small group of artifacts found north of the burials.

Comparative material for what has been referred to as the Titterington Focus (Titterington 1950:30, Editor's Note) is scarce. The Focus was defined on the basis of 10 sites in the St. Louis area of Illinois and Missouri. Another site in Missouri has subsequently been reported (Bacon and Miller 1957). All contained multiple burials covered with limestone slabs. A variety of point styles including Wadlow, Etley, and large side-notched plus other artifacts were associated with the burials (Table 7).

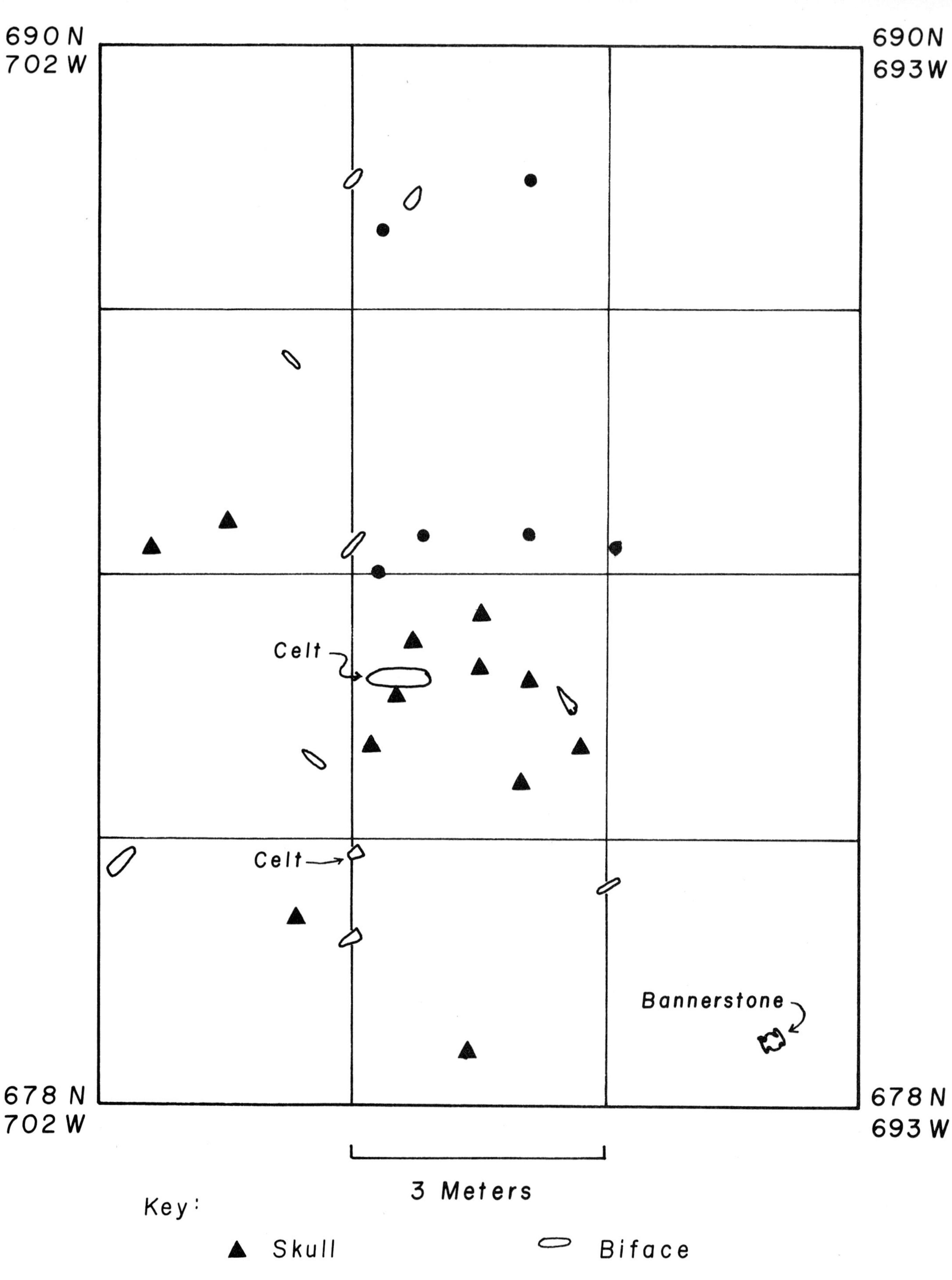

Figure 6. Mortuary goods in relation to skulls. The celt and bannerstone are labeled; other symbols are shown in the key.

TABLE 7

Assemblages from Titterington Focus Mortuary Sites

Artifacts and Other Characteristics	Etley	Kampsville	Marquette Park	Elm Point	Hartford Church	Gronefeld	Godar	Hemphill (3)	Weiman	Airport
Lanceolate Point	75	2	21	0	+	+	0	0	20	11
Etley Point	13	0	1	1	+	+			1	1
Turkey Tail Point				47						
Side-notched Point					+	?	+	1		1
Other Points					+	+	+			
Grooved Axes	25		2		7	3	25	1	6	
Bannerstones	3	2				1	24	1		1
Copper Artifacts	4	1						13		
Plummets				7			6	1		
Stone Celts						1				2
Bone/Antler					9					
Other Artifacts			3	1						
Burial Technique	E	?	E	?	?	?	E	?	B	B
Red Ochre	+	?	—	+	+	+	+	+	—	—
Limestone Slab	+	+	+	+	+	+	+	+	+	—
Number of Burials	24–54	?	2	?	?	?	?	3	40	13

Burial Technique:

   E—Extended
   B—Bundle

References:

Weiman Site (Bacon and Miller 1957).
All others, except Airport (Titterington 1950).

A number of problems occur with the taxonomy of the Late Archaic in central Illinois. White (1968:97–103) reexamined some of Titterington's material and grouped a series of sites on the basis of presence of Wadlow, Etley, and large side-notched points. Cook (n.d.:50), however, has defined a Titterington *Phase* including a group of sites defined by the presence of Wadlow, Etley, and/or Turkey Tail points and specifically excluding sites with side-notched points (n.d.:50). Although Cook includes the Airport Site in this phase (n.d.:60), it is clear that if we accept his definition the Airport Site should not be defined as a Titterington Phase site since it has a side-notched point. For present purposes comparison will be made with all eleven reported components and the term *Titterington Focus* will be used.

The problem of poor bone preservation plagues all reported Titterington Focus burials. However, two modes of burial seem to occur: bundle and extended. Titterington (1950) explicitly notes the presence of extended burials at the Etley and Marquette Park sites while Bacon and Miller (1957:21) similarly report bundle burials at the Weiman site. Wadlow and Etley points were found at all four sites. The Airport Site would, however, seem to be most like the Weiman Site, 23LN11 (Bacon and Miller 1957:21):

The area in which the burials occurred was quite irregular in outline but can roughly be described as a crude circle about eight feet in diameter, with an area about four feet in width and nineteen feet in length extending in a northeasterly direction from the circle. The burials had no specific distribution within the area but seemed to occur at random. . . . The long bones had been placed close to each other in all burials, and in several instances were placed side by side, with another group of long bones placed on top. The effect of this placement was to give the appearance of a careful stacking of the bones. From these observations it has been tentatively concluded that the bundle burial was the dominant practice of this group.

The major difference between the Airport Site and other reported components is the absence of limestone slabs among the burials at the Airport Site. The absence is probably not surprising, however, since limestone does not outcrop in the Sangamon River Valley as it does in the river valleys from which Titterington Focus mortuary sites are reported. Less conspicuous is the absence of red ochre, missing also at the Weiman and Marquette Park sites.

Mortuary sites are one site-type of the Titterington Focus. Cook (n.d.:66) has concluded that two types of habitation sites additionally are recognizable (within his Titterington Phase). These include short-term bivouacs and short-term base camps. Excavated and reported habitation components include the Booth (Klippel 1969) and

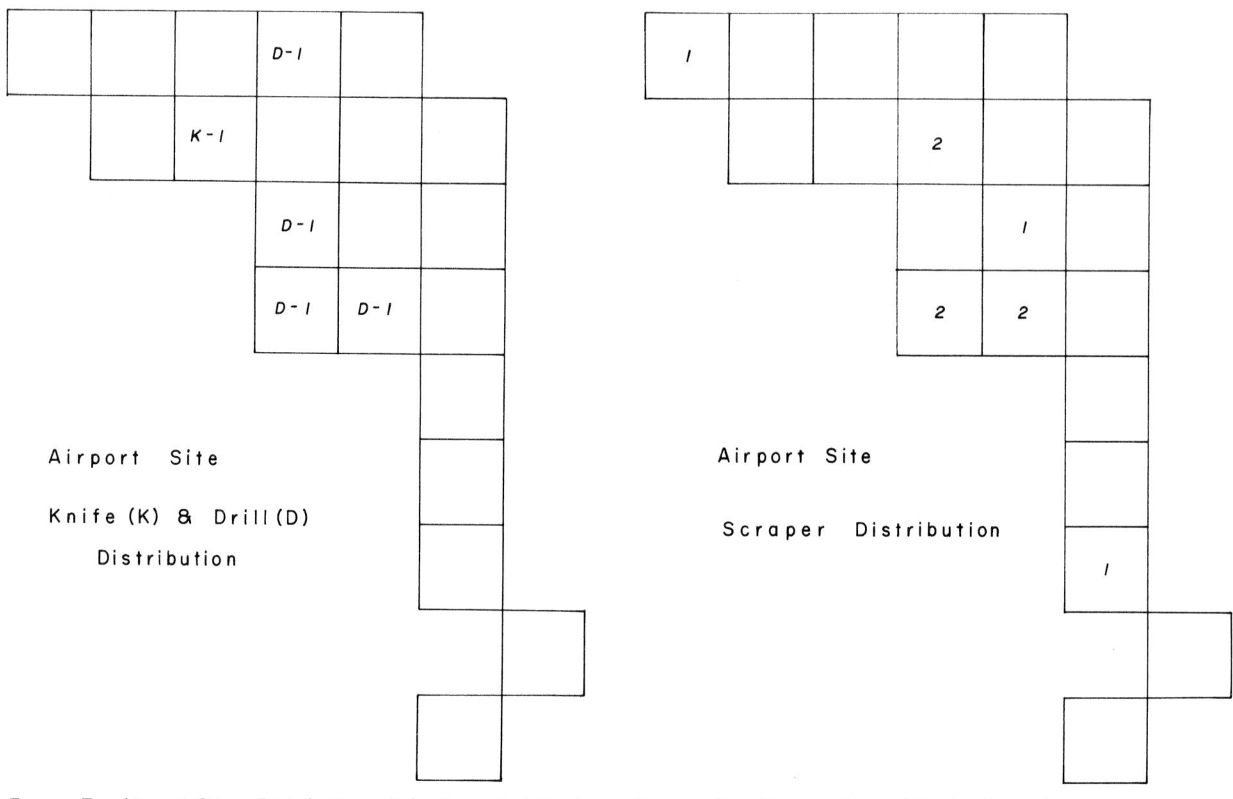

Figure 7. Airport Site: Distribution of knife and drills in test squares.

Figure 8. Airport Site: Distribution of scrapers in test squares.

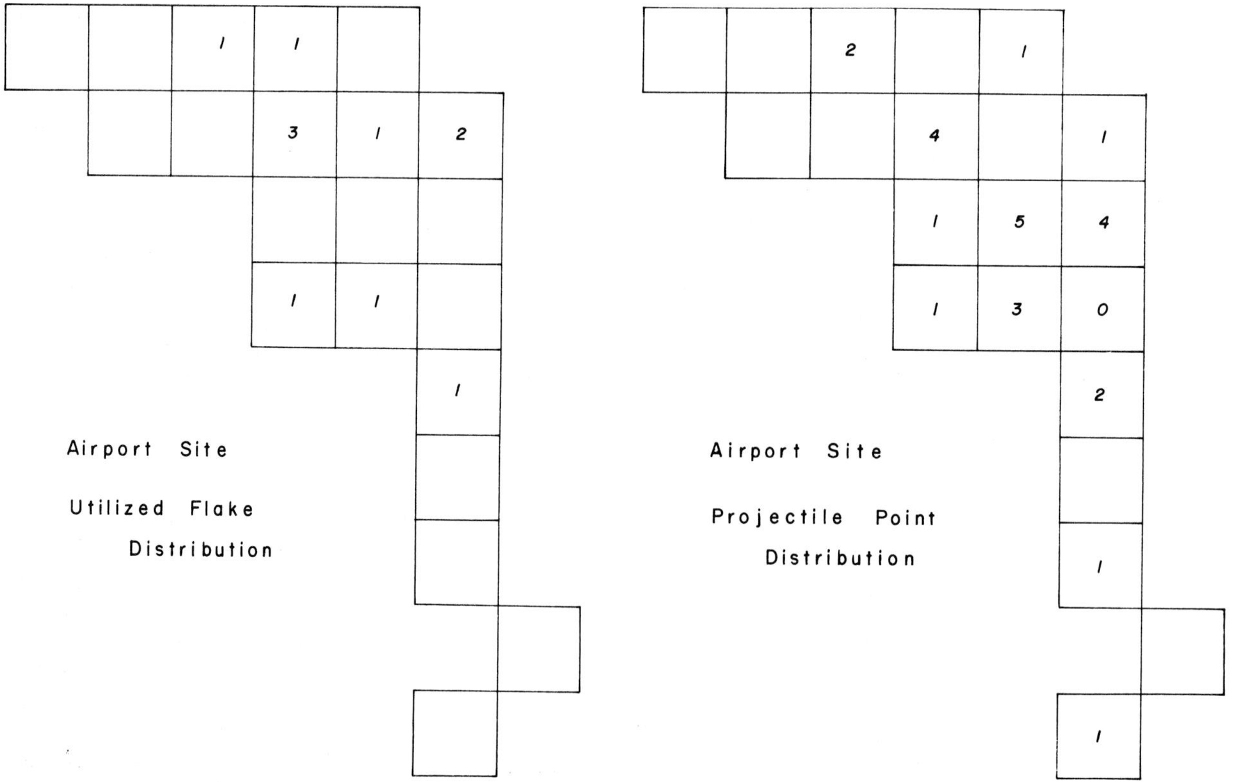

Figure 9. Airport Site: Distribution of utilized flakes in test squares.

Figure 10. Airport Site: Distribution of projectile points in test squares.

26

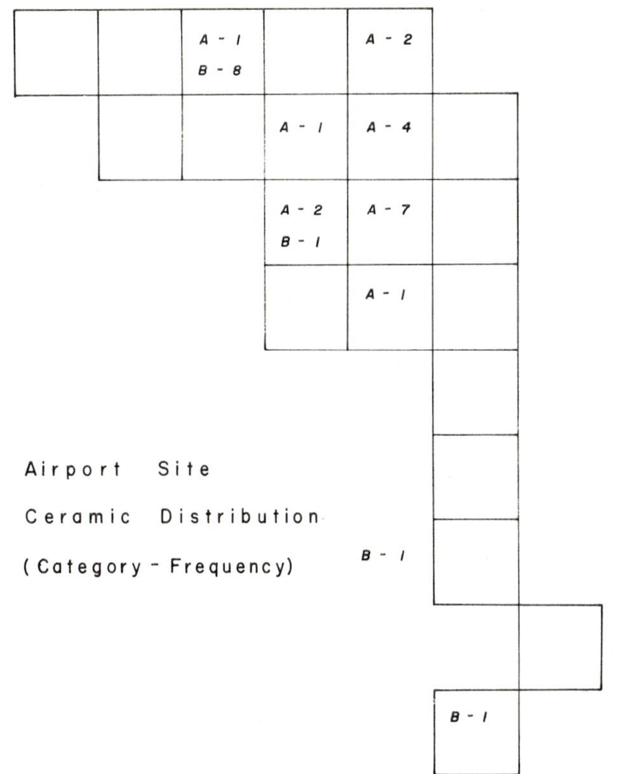

Figure 11. Airport Site: Distribution of ceramics (category-frequency) in test squares.

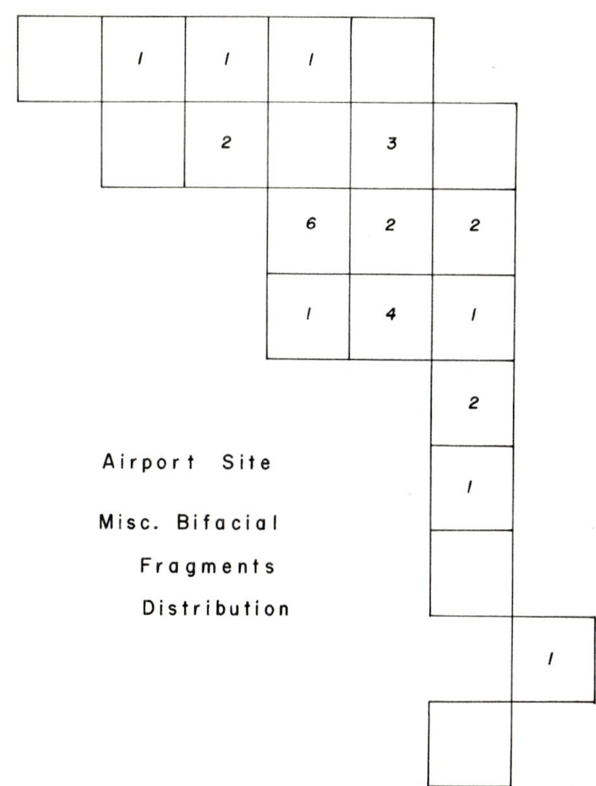

Figure 12. Airport Site: Distribution of miscellaneous bifacial fragments in test squares.

Hunt (Klippel n.d.) sites in Missouri, the Modoc Rock Shelter (Fowler 1959) and the Koster Site Horizon IV (Houart 1971, Cook n.d.) in Illinois, while some similar material (as well as much that is dissimilar) occurs at the Collins Site (Klippel 1972b) in Missouri. At all of these sites, the Titterington component is identified on the basis of the presence of Wadlow and/or Etley points.

Unfortunately, the Focus is poorly dated. A single radiocarbon date of 3950 ± 75 years B.P. (ISGS-329) is available for Koster Horizon IV (Cook n.d.:73). No other site has been radiometrically dated.

RIVERTON CULTURE

The remainder of the assemblage has been used to interpret the Airport Site as the locus, at several times, of a limited range of habitation activities. This interpretation is based on two major lines of positive evidence: the nature and contents of the tool assemblage and the nature of the debitage associated with these tools.

The chipped-stone tool assemblage, exclusive of the large mortuary bifaces, consisted of 36 projectile points or point parts, 2 bifacial knives, 10 scrapers, 4 drills, 4 manos, and 29 potsherds representing a minimum of 2 and maximum of

3 vessels. Distribution of this material in the excavations is shown in Figures 7 through 12. The heavy emphasis on procurement and processing implements, to the near exclusion of domestic equipment, argues for an interpretation of the Airport Site as having been a hunting camp or at least as never having been the locus of prolonged occupation.

Since the present analysis employed Winters' functional approach to describe tools, it is appropriate to go one step further with this approach and apply his site-function index to the Airport Site assemblage. The index is a ratio of fabricating, processing, and domestic tools to weapons (Winters 1969:131):

> The hypothesis, here, was simply that if the sites actually differ in their functions, then these differences should be reflected in the proportions of the various functional categories of the artifacts present in the . . . sites.

In the Riverton settlement system, "settlements" should have ratios from about 4.0 to 8.0, "transient camps" about 2.0, "base camps" about 1.0, "specialized hunting camps" about 0.5, and "generalized hunting camps" from 0 to 0.2 (Winters 1969:137). Disregarding the Titterington material, calculation of the Systemic Index gives a ratio of 0.22 if we also disregard ceramics or 0.28 if we give ceramics a value of 2 for minimum number of vessels. This value falls well within Winters' expected range for hunting camps but somewhere between the values for specialized and generalized camps.

Two dangers are inherent in using the Systemic Index at the Airport Site: (1) the realization that several discrete occupations are responsible for the presence of the material used to compute the ratio, and (2) the possibility that the sample could be biased both by prehistoric removal of useful tools (what Binford [1973:242] has referred to as "curation" behavior), and by recent collector activity. It will be shown below that there is no reason to believe that either of the two habitation occupations was significantly different from one another. Further, we suspect that historic disturbance of the Airport Site deposits has been minimal. The presence of large bifacial tools *on the surface* may suggest that collectors did not know of the site, and the fact that nearly all broken biface segments were matched further argues in favor of little disturbance other than from Euro-American agricultural activity.

The possibility of the sample being skewed by the prehistoric inhabitants of the site is not a problem unique to the Airport Site, and the present interpretation is supported by examination of the debitage. It might be expected that this unmodified waste material has been little disturbed and might be a rather more accurate reflection of prehistoric activity (cf. Schiffer 1972).

The debitage analysis examined both the kind and size of the flakes. Only 11 retouched and/or utilized flakes were found, compared with 1761 unmodified flakes. Thus, less than one percent of the flakes found at the site showed evidence of modification by either retouch or use. This would seem to indicate little casual use of by-products of the manufacturing process. In a similar analysis, Gregg (1974:241–243) tabulated the percentage of utilized edges on flakes from three Havana habitation sites in northwestern Illinois (Henderson County). He found that 41.7 to 79.7 percent of potentially utilizable edge quadrants were actually used. On the other hand, tabulation of flake types at the Airport Site indicates the presence of 33 bifacial retouch flakes (1.9% of the unmodified flakes).

The debitage was also size-graded through two nested screens, one of ½-inch mesh, one of ¼-inch mesh. The majority (87%) of the flakes passed through the ½-inch but not the ¼-inch screen (Table 5). Although the lack of primary chert sources in the Sangamon Valley forced the prehistoric inhabitant to rely on either imported cherts or cobbles from glacial tills and stream beds, the small size of most flakes again suggests that later stages in the manufacturing process predominated at the Airport Site.

In sum, both the tools and the debitage recovered at the Airport Site argue for an interpretation of a limited range of extractive and maintenance activities at the site. Processing and domestic activities are poorly represented.

"Limited activity" habitation occupations at two periods of time may be isolated. A component representative of the Riverton Culture, as defined by Winters (1969), is recognized on the basis of small projectile points typologically similar to those defined as diagnostic of the Riverton Culture and by the presence of two bifacially worked knives, also typologically similar to Riverton Culture specimens.

If we compare this meager list with the description of the Riverton Culture by Winters (1969), it is apparent that the Airport Site assemblage corresponds rather closely with the hunting camp type of site defined by Winters (1967:30; 1969:110). Winters notes that his survey of the Wabash River valley in Illinois located 22 sites which could be identified as Riverton Culture sites only by the presence of diagnostic points. The sites are described as covering only a few hundred square feet, lacking mussel shell (Winters 1969:110) and having only projectile points and blades as definite implements (Winters 1969:125).

Major components of the Riverton Culture appear to be confined primarily to an area about 500 mi², only about half of which was intensively utilized, in the central Wabash Valley. Hunting camps are, however, recognized by Winters (1969:110) as being somewhat more widely dispersed:

> We have received reports, . . ., that there are hunting camps with Riverton Culture points some 80 miles north of the Riverton Site on the Wabash River. These sites are described as being small, without mussel shell, and lacking all other artifacts of the Riverton Culture. Perhaps these represent a wide dispersal into seasonal hunting camps . . .

It is clear from work done in Illinois since Winters' work in the Wabash Valley that Riverton hunting camps are even more widely dispersed. Comparisons may be made with two such components—the Koster Site in the lower Illinois River valley and the Radford Site in the Sangamon River valley.

A small but apparently rather intense Riverton component appears in the third horizon of the Koster Site (Houart 1971:30–31). Projectile points diagnostic of the Riverton Culture, plus a small bifacial tool (not illustrated by Houart), were the only artifacts recovered from the 1969 excavations in Horizon III at Koster. Subsequent excavations have not yet been published. Houart (1971:31) suggests that Koster Horizon III may have been a Riverton Culture hunting camp at which a considerable amount of chipped stone manufacture and/or repair might have taken place.

Similarly, at the Radford Site (11Sg^{v}128) on the Sangamon River bluff 7.8 km upriver from the Airport Site, surface collections made by the Illinois State Museum in 1971 recovered projectile points similar to Riverton Culture types, plus a drill, several small knives, and a large amount of chipping debris. Although Radford too is multicomponent, the Riverton material is prominent within the assemblage. Coring with a one-inch soil probe suggested that Radford, like Airport, is no deeper than the plowzone.

Winters (1969:110) notes that his 22 hunting camps were located on the T-1 of the Wabash; however, the distribution of forest and prairie in the Wabash Valley was not delineated in relation to these sites. In any event, the two Sangamon Valley Riverton hunting camps (Airport and Radford) are both located just back of the crest of the low south bluff of the Sangamon River, on sandy soils, and near the prairie/forest ecotone. In such positions, their inhabitants would have been in an ideal location to hunt animals such as deer—apparently the meat staple of the Riverton Culture (Parmalee 1969:139).

MIDDLE/LATE WOODLAND

The final component isolated at the Airport Site is a Middle/Late Woodland occupation represented by at least two but no more than three ceramic vessels and by at least one projectile point. One reworked scraper is made on a point type found in the Middle to Late Woodland periods; and while this does not date the scraper, it at least provides a *terminus a quo* for its deposition. Since only three small rim sherds were collected, the two ceramic vessels were difficult to identify. Tentative identifications, however, place them in the late Middle Woodland/early Late Woodland time range.

The identification of the Category A rim is made with some confidence since it closely fits the definition of Weaver Ware. If this identification is correct, it is the furthermost upstream Weaver sherd yet found in the Sangamon Valley. The other rim, Category B, is perhaps somewhat more tentatively identified. We have, however, remarked that paste and temper suggest

Havana. Wittry (1959:209) describes a type of pottery in southwestern Wisconsin, Denzer Stamped, characterized by cord-marking over the entire body, although the neck may be smooth, and with cord-wrapped-stick impressions on the interior of the rim. Hurley (1974) similarly recognized this characteristic at Silver Creek Site 1 also in southwestern Wisconsin. Less than a half dozen similar examples have been identified among over 1,000 Havana rim sherds collected in the Sangamon River valley. Wittry remarks (1959:253–254) that Denzer Stamped in Wisconsin "resembles the Havana Ware pottery of Illinois, particularly its later variants."

Distribution of ceramics is illustrated in Figure 8, showing them to generally be somewhat northwest of the mortuary material. The exact horizontal provenience of the Steuben point is uncertain as it was picked up on the surface prior to excavations.

A basic functional differentiation of Woodland sites in central Illinois has been well recognized for many years. Mortuary sites, particularly mounds, and large habitation sites have occupied the attention of archaeologists in Illinois since at least the 1930s. It has been only in recent years that hunting camps have been recognized in central Illinois as a distinct type of site in the late Middle Woodland/early Late Woodland settlement system.

A recent study of Woodland settlement patterns in the Sangamon drainage (Roper 1975) clearly recognized small hunting camps, generally identifiable as Woodland only by the presence of projectile points. These hunting camps were normally located within the uplands, usually near the prairie/forest ecotone. They are known throughout the drainage.

Similarly, Farnsworth (1973:34), Gardner (1969:160), and Munson, Parmalee, and Yarnell (1971:429) have recognized the presence of Woodland hunting camps in the uplands of the Macoupin Creek, upper Kaskaskia River, and lower Spoon River, respectively.

No such site, to our knowledge, has been excavated although, of course, sites on the upland plain will generally be shallow. It was hoped that the Airport Site might give some information about the structure of the remains of such a site. The results are only partially useful since the presence of two Late Archaic components precludes identification of which material (other than pottery and one point) is Woodland. Certainly nothing seems to contradict the functional interpretation of a hunting camp, however. The presence of two ceramic vessels should not seriously alter the conclusion.

SUMMARY AND CONCLUSIONS

The Airport Site was a locus for prehistoric activity at three different times. Its first use was the burial of 13 individuals by Late Archaic Titterington Focus people. All but one (or possibly two) of these interments consisted of bundled bones. Chipped stone bifaces, celts, and a bannerstone were included among the burials. Although similar in content to a number of other known sites in Illinois and Missouri, the Airport Site is geographically far from any of them. Its presence in the Sangamon Valley thus expands the known range of the Titterington Focus. It should be noted, however, that taxonomy of west-central Illinois and northeastern Missouri Late Archaic mortuary components is in need of clarification.

At some later date, the same sand ridge on the south crest of the Sangamon River bluff was briefly occupied by Riverton Culture people. Activities carried out at this locus were apparently limited and possibly reflect the remains of a camp briefly occupied during a hunting foray into the Sangamon River area. The physiographic location of the site would indeed be ideal for maximally efficient hunting nearby. The Airport Site is one of a small number of such camps known outside the Wabash River Valley. It is not, however, the only known Riverton Culture hunting camp in the Sangamon Valley.

The final prehistoric occupation was by late Middle/early Late Woodland people. The nature of this occupation was probably similar to that of the Riverton Culture occupation. The physiographic position of the site again would be ideal for hunting, and the location corresponds to that identified for numerous other Middle Woodland and Weaver phase camps in the Sangamon Valley (cf. Roper 1975).

Late Archaic mortuary sites have been studied in Illinois for over a quarter of a century. The Airport Site was, therefore, not unique in this respect. It is unfortunate that bone preservation at many Late Archaic mortuary sites is poor.

Excavation of hunting camps is, however, rare. Although the recognition of such components in models of settlement systems is beginning, investigations of such sites are few. The excavations at the Airport Site were thus productive in information concerning the contents of such camps.

LITERATURE CITED

Ahler, Stanley A.
1971 Projectile Point Form and Function at Rodgers Shelter, Missouri. *Missouri Archaeological Society Research Series,* No. 8. Columbia.

Anderson, Adrienne B.
1975 "Least Cost" Strategy and Limited Activity Site Location in the Upper Dry Cimarron River Valley, Northeastern New Mexico. Ph.D. Dissertation, University of Colorado, Boulder.

Bacon, Willard S. and William J. Miller
1957 Notes on the Excavation of a Burial Area in Northeast Missouri. *The Missouri Archaeologist,* Vol. 19, No. 3, pp. 19–33.

Bass, William M.
1971 *Human Osteology: A Laboratory and Field Manual of the Human Skeleton.* Columbia, Missouri Archaeological Society.

Binford, Lewis R.
1973 "Interassemblage Variability—the Mousterian and the 'Functional' Argument." *In* The Explanation of Culture Change: Models in Prehistory, Colin Renfrew (Ed.), pp. 227–254. Pittsburgh, University of Pittsburgh Press.

Brose, David S.
1975 Functional Analysis of Stone Tools: A Cautionary Note on the Role of Animal Fats. *American Antiquity,* Vol. 40, No. 1, pp. 86–94.

Campbell, John
1968 "Territoriality Among Ancient Hunters: Interpretations from Ethnography and Nature." *In* Anthropological Archeology in the Americas, Betty J. Meggers (Ed.), pp. 1–21, Washington, D.C., Anthropological Society of Washington.

Chapman, Carl H.
1975 *The Archaeology of Missouri,* I. Columbia, University of Missouri Press.

Chapman, Jefferson
1975 The Rose Island Site and the Bifurcate Point Tradition. *University of Tennessee, Department of Anthropology, Reports of Investigations,* No. 14. Knoxville.

Cook, Thomas G.
n.d. Koster: An Artifact Analysis of Two Archaic Phases in West-Central Illinois. Ph.D. Dissertation, University of Chicago.

Farnsworth, Kenneth B.
1973 An Archaeological Survey of the Macoupin Valley. *Illinois State Museum Reports of Investigations,* No. 26, *Illinois Valley Archaeological Program Research Papers,* Vol. 7. Springfield.

Fowler, Melvin L.
1957 The Ferry Archaic Site, Hardin County, Illinois. *Illinois State Museum Scientific Papers,* Vol. VIII, No. 1. Springfield.
1959 Summary Report of the Modoc Rock Shelter, 1952, 1953, 1955, 1956. *Illinois State Museum Reports of Investigations,* No. 8, Springfield.

Frison, George
1968 A Functional Analysis of Certain Chipped Stone Tools. *American Antiquity,* Vol. 33, No. 2, pp. 149–155.

Gardner, William M.
1969 The Havana Cultural Tradition Occupation in the Upper Kaskaskia River Valley, Illinois. Ph.D. Dissertation, University of Illinois, Urbana. Ann Arbor, University Microfilms.

Gregg, Michael L.
1974 Three Middle Woodland Sites from Henderson County: An Apparent Congruity with Middle Woodland Subsistence-Settlement Systems in the Lower Illinois Valley. *The Wisconsin Archeologist,* Vol. 55, No. 3, pp. 231–245.

Griffin, James B.
1952 "Some Early and Middle Woodland Pottery Types." *In* Hopewellian Communities in Illinois, Thorne Deuel (Ed.), *Illinois State Museum Scientific Papers,* Vol. V, pp. 93–130, Springfield.

Houart, Gail L.
1971 Koster: A Stratified Archaic Site in the Illinois Valley. *Illinois State Museum Reports of Investigations,* No. 22, *Illinois Valley Archaeological Program Research Papers,* Vol. 4, Springfield.

Hurley, William M.
1974 Silver Creek Woodland Sites, Southwestern Wisconsin. *Office of the State Archaeologist Report,* No. 6. Iowa City, The University of Iowa.

Johnson, Judith B.
n.d. Proto-Euro-American Phytogeography of the Lower Sangamon River Drainage. Manuscript and maps on file, Anthropology Department, Illinois State Muesum, Springfield.

Judge, W. James
1973 *PaleoIndian Occupation of the Central Rio Grande Valley of New Mexico.* Albuquerque, University of New Mexico Press.

Klippel, Walter E.
1969 The Booth Site: A Late Archaic Campsite. *Missouri Archaeological Society Research Series,* No. 6. Columbia.
1972a Cultural Adaptation to Post-Pleistocene Environments in the Illinois Prairie Peninsula. Report to the National Science Foundation, Grant GS-28986.
1972b An Early Woodland Period Manifestation in the Prairie Peninsula. *Journal of the Iowa Archaeological Society,* Vol. 19.
n.d. The Hunt Site. Ms.

Knoblock, Byron W.
1939 *Bannerstones of the North American Indian.* LaGrange, Illinois, Byron W. Knoblock.

Miller, James A.
1973 Quaternary History of the Sangamon River Drainage System, Central Illinois. *Illinois State Museum Reports of Investigations,* No. 27. Springfield.

Morse, Dan F.
1963 The Steuben Village and Mounds: A Multicomponent Site in Illinois. *University of Michigan Anthropological Papers,* No. 21. Ann Arbor.

Munson, Patrick J., Paul W. Parmalee, and Richard A. Yarnell
1971 Subsistence Ecology of Scovill, A Terminal Middle Woodland Village. *American Antiquity,* Vol. 36, No. 4, pp. 410–431.

Parmalee, Paul W.
1969 Animal Remains from the Archaic Riverton, Swan Island, and Robeson Hills Sites, Illinois. Appendix to: The Riverton Culture. *Illinois State Museum Reports of Investigations,* No. 13. Springfield.

Perino, Gregory
1968 Guide to the Identification of Certain American Indian Projectile Points. *Oklahoma Anthropological Society Special Bulletin,* No. 3. Norman.

Plog, Fred T.
1974   *The Study of Prehistoric Change.* New York, Academic Press.
Redman, Charles A. and Patty Jo Watson
1970   Systematic, Intensive Surface Collection. *American Antiquity,* Vol. 35, No. 3, pp. 279–291.
Ritzenthaler, Robert
1946   The Osceola Site—an Old Copper Site near Potosi, Wisconsin. *The Wisconsin Archeologist,* Vol. 27, No. 3.
Roper, Donna C.
1975   Archaeological Survey and Settlement Pattern Models in Central Illinois. Ph.D. Dissertation, University of Missouri, Columbia.
1976   Lateral Displacement of Artifacts Due to Plowing. *American Antiquity,* Vol. 41, No. 3, pp. 372–375.
Schiffer, Michael B.
1972   Archaeological Context and Systemic Context. *American Antiquity,* Vol. 37, No. 2, pp. 156–165.
Scully, Edward G.
1951   Some Central Mississippi Valley Projectile Point Types. University of Michigan, Museum of Anthropology. Mimeographed.
Struever, Stuart
1968   Woodland Subsistence-Settlement Systems in the Lower Illinois River Valley. *In* New Perspectives in Archeology, Sally R. Binford and Lewis R. Binford (Eds.), pp. 285–312. Chicago, Aldine.
Titterington, Paul F.
1950   Some Non-Pottery Sites in St. Louis Area. *Illinois State Archaeological Society Journal,* Vol. I, No. 1, (N.S.), pp. 19–31.

Vehik, Rain
1974   Archaeological Investigations in the Harry S. Truman Reservoir Area: 1970. Report to the National Park Service. University of Missouri, Columbia.
Webb, William S.
1974   *Indian Knoll.* Knoxville, Univ. of Tennessee Press.
White, Anta M.
1968   The Lithic Industries of the Illinois Valley in the Early and Middle Woodland Period. *University of Michigan Anthropological Papers,* No. 35. Ann Arbor.
Willman, H. B. and John C. Frye
1970   Pleistocene Stratigraphy of Illinois. *Illinois State Geological Survey Bulletin* 94. Urbana.
Wilmsen, Edwin N.
1970   Lithic Analysis and Cultural Inference: A Paleo-Indian Case. *Anthropological Papers,* No. 16. Tucson, University of Arizona Press.
Winters, Howard D.
1967   An Archaeological Survey of the Wabash Valley in Illinois. *Illinois State Museum Reports of Investigations,* No. 10. Springfield.
1969   The Riverton Culture. *Illinois State Museum Reports of Investigations,* No. 13. Springfield.
Wittry, Warren
1959   The Raddatz Rockshelter, SK5, Wisconsin. *The Wisconsin Archeologist,* Vol. 40, No. 2, pp. 33–69.
Wray, Donald E. and Richard S. MacNeish
1961   The Hopewellian and Weaver Occupations of the Weaver Site, Fulton County, Illinois. *Illinois State Museum Scientific Papers,* Vol. VIII, No. 2. Springfield.